Mt. Omei
To Chengdu
Leshan
Omei
Mt. Minya Gongka
To Yaan
Fulin
Dadu River
Obian
Mabian
Yuexi
Mianning
Xikang
Lugu
Yangzi River
Lizhou
Zhaojue
Xichang
Qionghai
Lake
Dechang
Anning River
Huili
To Kunming
River of Golden Sand
Independent
Nosuland
Salawu
Yunnan
Roads
Trails
35 mile to 1 inch

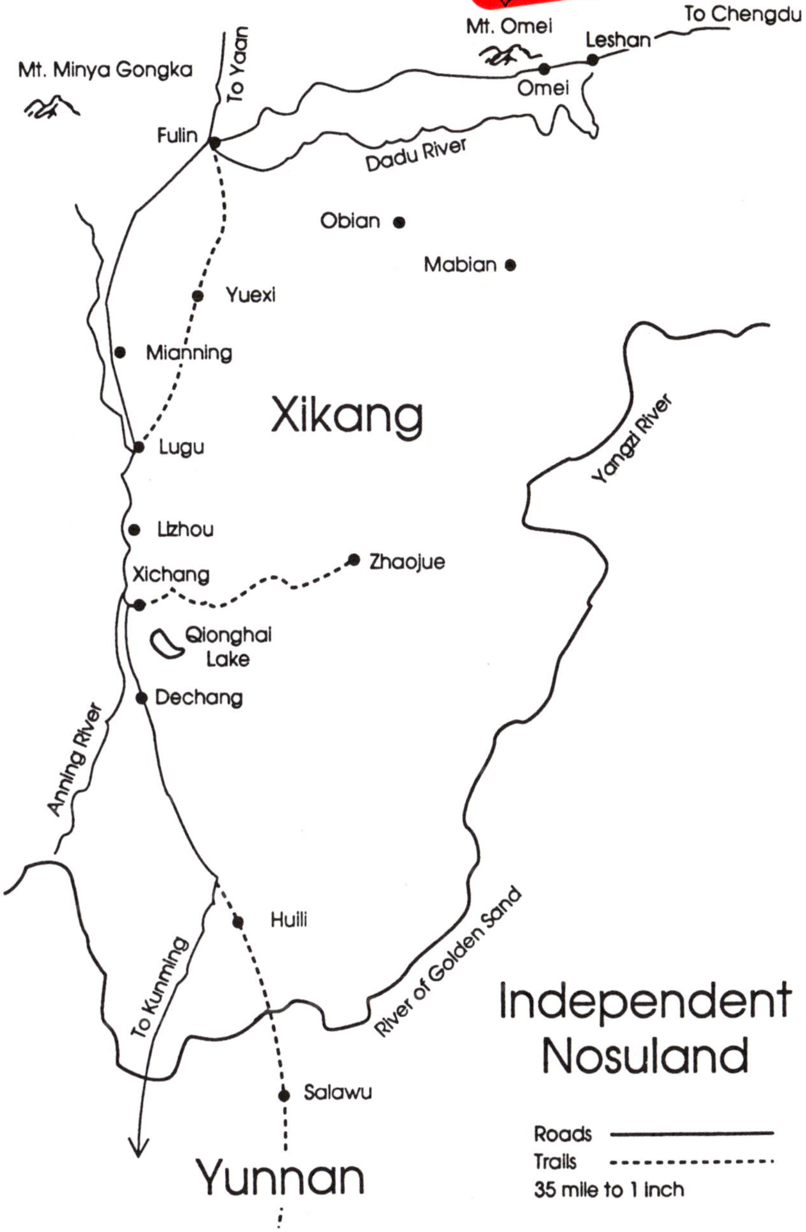

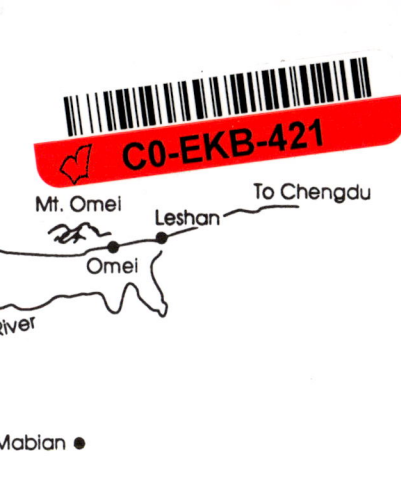

Me? A Missionary?

The Saga of a First Term Missionary

Dan and Lucille Carr at the end of their first term of service in China.

Me? A Missionary?

The Saga of a First Term Missionary

Daniel L. Carr

John S. Begley, Illustrator
Foreword by Ralph Covell

Unless otherwise noted, all Scripture quotations in this book are from the *New American Standard Bible*,© 1960, 1962, 1963, 1968, 1971, 1972, 1973, 1975, 1977, by the Lockman Foundation. Used by permission.

Some Scripture quotations in this publication are from the *New King James Version*. Copyright © 1979, 1980, 1982, Thomas Nelson, Inc., Publishers.

Scripture quotations marked (NIV) are taken from the *Holy Bible, New International Version*. Copyright ©1973, 1978, 1984, International Bible Society. Used by permission of Zondervan Bible Publishers.

Illustrator: John S. Begley
Manuscript Editor: Walter G. Opyd

FIRST EDITION

All rights reserved, including the right of reproduction in whole or in part in any form.

Copyright © 1991 by Daniel L. Carr

Published by Vantage Press, Inc.
516 West 34th Street, New York, New York 10001

Manufactured in the United States of America
ISBN: 0-533-09367-8

Library of Congress Catalog Card No.: 90-91398

0 9 8 7 6 5 4 3 2 1

DEDICATION

To Lucille, my loving wife and faithful companion in the service of Jesus Christ, and to my children who shared our experiences in China.

CONTENTS

Foreword   xi
Acknowledgments   xiii
Preface   xv

Chapter

1. "The Lord Called"   1
2. "I Said, 'Here am I. Send Me!'"   13
3. "The Lord Said, 'Go to the Land Which I Will Show You'"   19
4. "Being Recommended by the Brethren"   25
5. "And Accompanied unto the Ship"   33
6. "I Came Into Asia"   39
7. "It is a Land of Idols"   53
8. "I Tarry in the Plain"   59
9. "To be Expert in All Customs"   67
10. "I am Restless in My Complaint"   75
11. "I Heard a Language that I did not Know"   81
12. "And Behold, There was a Basket of Summer Fruit"   87
13. "As for the Western Border"   107
14. "The Harvest is Plentiful, but the Laborers are Few"   123
15. "I, Daniel, was Exhausted and Sick"   133
16. "Then I got Up Again and Carried on the King's Business"   143
17. "On the Mountains"   159
18. "In the Presence of My Enemies"   171
19. "The Commissioners Began Trying to Find a Ground of Accusation Against Daniel"   183
20. "I was Found Innocent"   209
21. "He then Brought Me out through the Gate Facing East"   219

Pinyin Alphabet Pronunciation Guide   233

FOREWORD

The modern missionary era in China came to a sudden halt in 1949. Deprived of outside money, advice, and help in evangelism, God's people in China, even in adverse circumstances, embarked on a period of growth never previously seen in that country. It became a truly Chinese Church able to identify with and penetrate its own culture.

During these "post-liberation" years, the term "missionary" has not been a popular one in China. It smacked too much of old imperialistic attitudes that had shackled the Christian Church with the millstone of "foreign." Since the time of the cultural revolution (1966-1976), often called "years of chaos" by the Chinese, there has been a growing appreciation in China for missionaries as people—their commitment, their concern, and their care for their adopted home.

Dan Carr is one of those missionaries. His interest in doing God's will did not begin with China. Evangelism was his heart from the time of his conversion. The Navy Chaplaincy gave him the opportunity to serve both his country and his Lord. China had no more spiritual need than his own America, but this is where he felt God wanted him to continue his Christian service.

I have known Dan and his wife, Lucille, from the time when they were fellow students with me at Eastern Baptist Seminary in Philadelphia. Later I was among that group of Baptist missionaries who served with the Carrs along the border of Eastern Tibet. Following this, my wife and I were to serve with them in Taiwan. They are numbered among our closest friends.

This book, *Me? A Missionary?*, is a welcome addition to a growing number of reflective books on the missionary enterprise in China. Missionary commitment was constantly tested. Living in an isolated area of China, the Carrs faced incredible odds: warring struggles among rival military lords, an opium-infested land, the perils of Communist "liberation," resistance to the Gospel message, and severe problems of personal health. Frank and honest, this account is filled with humor, descriptive vignettes of Chinese life, and enough personal detail to motivate many young people to join the next generation of missionaries.

Ralph Covell, Academic Dean
Denver Conservative Baptist Seminary

ACKNOWLEDGMENTS

One of the biggest blessings I've had in writing this book is the fellowship that I've enjoyed with my dear friend, John S. Begley, who illustrated the book. He is a very talented and dedicated Christian artist who has made very good use of his God-given gift. His drawings and beautiful oil paintings have brightened up a number of homes and business establishments.

John was a staff artist at the Mare Island Navy Yard in Vallejo, California, during World War II. His drawings can be seen in the National Geographic Magazine and other publications. Later he took on the task of drawing Christian comic books for the Union Gospel Press in Cleveland, Ohio. As time went on, he became a free lance artist and started his own lithographic business. One of his customers was Kresky Signs, Inc. Many of his drawings were seen on billboards in the western part of the country. John also worked for the Pischoff Art Department in San Francisco and drew sketches of courtroom trials for KGO Television in the same city. He did the sketches for the trial of Black Panther leader, Huey Newton.

John was Art Director for World Vision Magazine and for a number of years was Art Director for Marine World / Africa USA in Belmont, California. He is now enjoying the rewards of retirement at his home in Guerneville, California, where art students and art teachers from Sonoma State University come to his studio for lessons and advice.

I am very grateful to John for illustrating this book and especially grateful for the deep spiritual influence that he and his devoted wife, Juliet, have had on Lucille and me during the many years that we have known them. May God richly bless them.

I would also like to express my deep appreciation to Dr. Wally Opyd and his dear wife, Nancy, who spent many hours preparing this manuscript for publication.

Dan Carr
San Jose, California

PREFACE

"Why did you come here to tell us about this man Jesus?" The one who asked me this question was a little ten-year-old boy who just happened to be the Panchen Lama of Tibet. That was over forty years ago and, since that time, many others in West China and in Taiwan asked me that very same question. My answer was and still is, "I came here to tell you about this man Jesus because He himself called me to this task."

I would like to share with you some of the experiences I had while trying to carry out this task. This sharing might help some of you understand a little better some of the things involved in the development of a missionary and cause you to pray more intelligently for that missionary. It could be that some of you are preparing for foreign missionary service. If so, this saga of a first-term missionary might help you learn from his mistakes when you reach the field.

Some of the experiences that I will share with you were humorous. Others were difficult. Some were very discouraging. In fact, there were some that caused me to wonder why I was even trying to carry the Gospel of Jesus Christ to people whose culture was so different from mine, but I could not forget that CALL!

Me? A Missionary?

The Saga of a First Term Missionary

Chapter 1

"THE LORD CALLED"

"The Lord called Samuel again for the third time. And he arose and went to Eli, and said, 'Here I am, for you called me.' Then Eli discerned that the Lord was calling the boy." (1 Samuel 3:8)

Yes, the Lord called me, but it took three calls to produce my "Here I am" and my "Send me" was the result of no little amount of persuasion. Unlike that little boy whose readiness to answer the call gave old Eli a sleepless night, I tried to ignore the same. In my case, I thought it was a call to foreign missionary service and I didn't relish the idea one bit. There was more than enough for me to do at home. At least that was my excuse. The very thought of leaving home and country and burying myself in some far flung corner of the world was altogether unattractive, but the Lord continued to call.

Actually, the call first came before I was born. This may sound paradoxical, but it's true. My mother provides the proof. While in training for missionary work in the South Sea Islands as an Episcopalian deaconess, she met a young man. He fell in love with her and she fell in love with him. The result? He asked her hand in marriage. Now this presented a real problem, for good little deaconesses were not supposed to marry. What was the poor girl to do? Should she bury herself in work and mope around with a broken heart or marry the young fellow and bring down the wrath of her sister deaconesses? This was a question that called for the superintendent's advice.

"In love, eh? Well, what's so terribly wrong about falling in love?" was his response. "And who's the villain?"

"Oh, he's a nice young fellow from England, sir, and he's a good Christian!"

"A nice chap, eh? Well, ask him to drop in on me some time for a chat. I'd like to ask him a few questions."

In record time the visit was made. Soon after, my mother was called to the superintendent's office. Wasting no time in preliminaries, he said, "Young lady, my advice to you is marry that young man while you have the chance and raise a missionary." That's exactly what she felt led of the Lord to do, and it wasn't long before the wedding bells rang. Of course my dad was in full agreement with the superintendent's advice. Later, my mother gave birth to Ellen, Sidney, Paul, and Dorothy. Sidney went home to be with the Lord when he was just an infant. As each child appeared on the scene, my mother announced to her friends, "This is my missionary baby!"

It was on a very foggy day in 1917 that a new voice challenged the fog-horns out on San Francisco Bay. And what a voice! A relative came to the Mt. Zion Hospital in San Francisco to see the new arrival. She took one look at him and said to my mother, "Oh, the poor little thing. He's so frail. I wonder if he'll live."

Certainly this little bundle of noise and ugliness couldn't be that long-awaited missionary, but such was the case. The Lord called the older children into other fields of service; but in my case, "He who had set me apart, even from my mother's womb, and called me through His grace, was pleased to reveal His Son in me, that I might preach Him among the Gentiles" (Gal. 1:15,16). It also pleased the Lord to give my mother another child, William, who felt the call to pastor churches here in America.

Of course there was nothing I could do about this first call. That was in the hands of the Lord and my mother. As I grew older and finally entered high school, others entered the picture. One of them was my good friend, John Begley, who was intent on my making a decision for Jesus Christ. I, at the time, wasn't too much interested in making such a decision, but the Lord was. After all, if He was calling me to be a witness for Him, how could I witness for Him if I didn't know Him?

My parents were also anxious for me to become a Christian. As a child, I was expected to accompany them to services on Sunday. It was often a frightening time for me since the pastor, Rev. O. F. Goettel, was a minister of the Jonathan Edwards type. He was not afraid to preach about the wrath of God as well as the love of God.

There was another minister in the church who was made in the same mold and often substituted for Rev. Goettel. His name was Charles Winans, an old Indian fighter who had once captured, single-handedly, the famous Indian chief Geronimo when he escaped from an American military prison in Arizona. I can still see that dear old Christian soldier, with his distinguished mustache, standing up there time after time, waving his handkerchief and warning us about the fires of Hell. What a joy it was many years later when his great grandson, Robert Bryant, became my son-in-law.

Old Jonathan Edwards was not the only one who could preach about "Sinners in the Hands of an Angry God!" The sermons preached by O. F. Goettel and Charles Winans were just as powerful as the ones preached by Edwards during the American Revolution. Over and over again they would ask the question, "Are you saved or lost?" I had no problem when it came to the meaning of the word "lost." Anyone who was not saved was lost and bound for

"ME? A MISSIONARY?"

the fires of hell, but I was at a loss when it came to the meaning of the word "saved." Naturally, given the choice, I wanted to be saved. But what was involved in this process?

In our testimony meetings, members would try to explain the salvation process. Their testimonies usually followed the same line as the one given by a very dedicated lady in the church. Her testimony was always the same, "I'll never forget the day the Lord saved me. When I confessed my sins and believed in Him my life was changed completely, and I was filled with a joy that I can't explain. When I rose from my knees, I felt as though I was walking around on clouds. And as I left the church, everything appeared to be different. The people, the buildings, the trees seemed different."

The testimony of this lady made a real impression on me and I would often say to myself, "If that's what it means to be saved, then I want to be saved." Unfortunately, during the many times that I answered the "call to the altar," I never had such an experience and considered myself still lost.

As far as I knew, I had sincerely gone through all the motions. I had gotten down on my knees, truly confessed my sins, and believed with all my heart in Christ and in what He did for me on the Cross; but every time I got up from my knees, I didn't have the feeling that I was walking around on clouds. The unexplainable feeling of great joy was not there. And as I walked out of the church, everything was not different. Everything was still the same. The people, the buildings, and the trees were still the same.

When I was a senior in high school, I began to lose interest in spiritual things. Detecting this, John Begley again came to my rescue. This time he insisted that I attend a two-week series of evangelistic services at our church, the First Baptist Church of Petaluma, California, and he wouldn't take "No" for an answer. Well, I ended up by attending every service and when the invitation song was sung at the end of each service, I went forward to accept the Savior.

For thirteen days I went forward and for thirteen days the song leader, Herb Farrar, dealt with me as the evangelist, Ira Deal, and the pastor talked to other inquirers. Yes, for thirteen days I honestly did all that I thought I had to do to be saved. Result? No clouds. Not one solitary cloud. Not one thing was different. The buildings were still in need of repair and paint. The trees were still bare. The people were still the same. Not one of them looked like an angel. That feeling of overwhelming joy was still not in my heart, so I was more convinced than ever before that I was not saved.

On the fourteenth and last day of these special meetings, I responded again to the invitation. By this time, the song leader was just about ready to give up on me. Frustration was written all over his face. As he made one last attempt to help me, a dear old lady, Mrs. Shenicka, came down the aisle on the arm of her daughter who was already a dedicated Christian and sat at the other end of my pew as the evangelist dealt with her. So desperate was I to find salvation that I listened to what was going on at both ends of the pew. Suddenly, the daughter interrupted and said to the evangelist, "The trouble with my mother is that she's been waiting for a special feeling."

His immediate reply was, "My friend, we're not saved by feelings. Feelings are like the wind. They come and go. We are saved by taking God at His Word, and His Word tells us, 'If you confess with your mouth Jesus as Lord, and believe in your heart that God raised him from the dead, you shall be saved; for with the heart man believes, resulting in righteousness, and with the mouth he confesses, resulting in salvation'" (Rom. 10:9,10).

Suddenly, the old mother stood up with a smile on her face and calmly said, "God's Word tells me I'm saved, and so I am." At almost the same instant, I stood up and said the very same thing. Praise God! I was saved. I could take God's Word for it. My feelings had nothing to do with it. I was saved the very first time I sincerely confessed my sins and truly believed in Christ with all my heart. What I had lacked these many months was the assurance of salvation. For the first time, I had real peace and assurance in my heart.

It wasn't enough for John Begley to work and pray for my salvation. It wasn't long before he began pestering me with the thought of becoming a missionary. It was he who pointed his finger at me one day and said, "Dan, I think you should consider answering the missionary call." My response was, "ME? A MISSIONARY?"

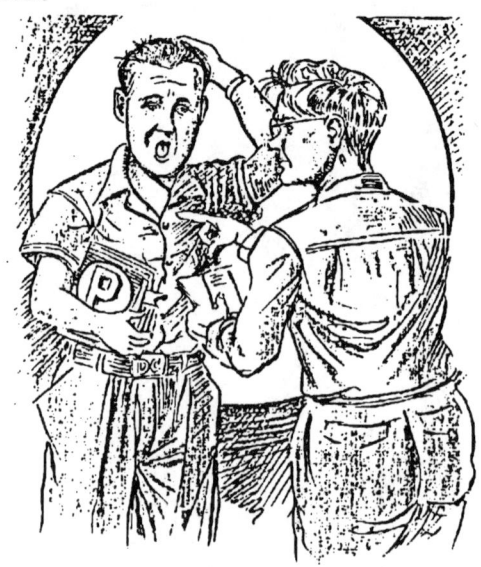

"THE LORD CALLED"

To this day I wonder why I didn't point my finger at him and say, "Perhaps you're the one who should answer the call." This I neglected to do and John went on to become an artist and illustrator of no small repute. As for me, I answered the call to the ministry.

My original career goal was to be a teacher of vocational agriculture and I hoped to gain admittance to the University of California in Davis, California, to begin studies toward this end. Since my father passed away soon after my graduation from Petaluma High School in 1935, I found it necessary to work on a ranch to secure funds for starting my college work.

My "aggie" teacher was a real friend and was determined to help me reach my goal. It was he who sent my transcript to Davis and accompanied it with a fine letter of recommendation.

My work on the ranch didn't require much in the way of brains, but it did require a lot of brawn. It meant leaving the bunkhouse at four in the morning, doing chores, working hard all day long, and finally heading for the bunkhouse at eight in the evening for my devotions and sleep. That was my schedule seven days a week. The pay was $25.00 per month with meals and a bunk. I was thankful to have six hours off on Sundays to attend church services in town.

The ranch offered me plenty of time to think and pray and ask God's guidance as I did my regular work. It wasn't long before I realized that God was calling me into the ministry. There was no walking around on clouds. No voice came to me out of the blue. There was just a real conviction that I should become a minister. Somehow I felt like Elisha who was plowing in a field when Elijah came and threw his prophet's cloak around him, indicating that he was passing on to him his prophetic power and authority. Elisha wasted no time in leaving his former occupation, saying farewell to his family, and following Elijah.

Like Elisha, I was actually plowing in a field when my teacher came walking out over the furrows and shouted to me, "Dan, you've been accepted as a student at the university. Will you be ready to leave for Davis this fall?" It was hard for me to muster up enough courage to tell him, "I've appreciated all that you've done for me, sir, but I'll not be going to Davis. I'll be studying for the ministry instead."

What a surprise I received when my old teacher put his hand on my shoulder and said, "Dan, if that's what God wants you to do, then do it. The biggest mistake I ever made was years ago when I felt God calling me to go to China as a missionary. I refused to answer that call and became a teacher of vocational agriculture instead. From that day to this, I have been a miserable man. God has punished me in so many ways."

I never thought the day would come when I would be counseling my teacher, but counsel him I did. Apparently that counseling came too late. As far as I know, he never did rededicate his life to the Lord. How glad I am that I did not take the course that he took. Instead, I took the course that led me to Baylor University in Waco, Texas, where I studied for the ministry. However, I still didn't see any relationship between the call to be a minister and the call to be a missionary.

Well, so much for my first call. The Lord called again when I was a budding young cleric deep down in the heart of Texas. So anxious was I to rock America with the Gospel that I left the rocking of the rest of the world to those who were more willing to sacrifice the best years of their lives in lands beyond the sea.

The Lord did bring a little of the mission field to me in the form of fellow college students who were the offspring of missionaries. Why did they have to keep chattering about the mission field? Why make such a fuss over lands so far away? Why did they keep bothering me about joining their Volunteer Missionary Band? How did they know that I was wrestling with the foreign mission call and trying to stay as far away from mission courses and mission books as possible? And what prompted my roommate to refer me to a little book called *The Splendor of God* by Honore Morrow? The only logical answer seemed to be wrapped up in the fact that God was still calling me.

The third and final call came during my first year at Eastern Baptist Theological Seminary in Philadelphia. By this time I was in that proverbial spiritual rut. Victorious Christian living was a thing of the past. I felt no power in prayer, little desire to witness, and my devotional life was often neglected. What a wretched "Jekyl and Hyde" existence. "For the good that I wish, I do not do; but I practice the very evil that I do not wish" (Romans 7:19). And to think that God had "counted me faithful, putting me into the ministry" (1 Timothy 1:12 KJV).

Despite this slough of despond, God was faithful and I found myself claiming the promise, "No temptation has seized you except what is common to man. And God is faithful; He will not let you be

"THE LORD CALLED"

tempted beyond what you can bear. But when you are tempted, He will also provide a way out so that you can stand up under it" (1 Cor. 10:13).

Things reached a climax early in 1941. Try as I would, I couldn't get away from those things having to do with Missions. There was that large missionary map ever before me in the school foyer, reminding me of the great spiritual need in other lands. There were also those unexpected talks in chapel on service overseas, required mission courses, and another group of missionary-minded students to hound me day and night.

Then came the explosion! As I broused through the seminary library, I noticed a book entitled *The Splendor of God*. Memory soon revealed that this was the book I neglected to read down in Texas. My roommate had never mentioned the contents of this book. He had merely recommended my reading it. For want of something better to do, I carried the book to my room and began to read it. Much to my surprise, I found myself lost in the life of Adoniram Judson; and, oddly enough, I had no desire to find my way out of it.

I saw Judson leave the shores of New England and followed him all the way to Burma, joined in his work, shared his sufferings, was touched by his dedication to missionary service, and at the end of the way—the last page and three o'clock in the morning—I fell on my knees and saw One greater than Judson. I caught a new glimpse of God's Son, Who loved me, and gave Himself for me. I saw Him leave His throne above and followed Him all the way to the Cross. The least I could do was take up my cross and follow Him. I've tried to explain what went on in my mind and heart in this bit of verse:

He Called Me

He called me once and called me thrice,
And oh! the bitter shame —
That I should pause to own His cause
And spread abroad His Name.

An easy post I wanted most
THERE to His will conform —
A faithful flock to share my stock
Of duties to perform.

But call He did and oft did bid
Me to His will resign;
Then, yielded o'er, I did implore,
"O, Lord, my soul refine!"

What a relief and joy it was to know that God was really calling me. In response to that call, it was only natural that "I said, 'Here am I. Send me!'"

"THE LORD CALLED"

Chapter 2

"I SAID, 'HERE AM I. SEND ME!'"

"I heard the voice of the Lord, saying, 'Whom shall I send, and who will go for Us?' Then I said, 'Here am I. Send me!'" (Isaiah 6:8)

It was not until I used Isaiah's response to God's call and said, "Here am I; send me," that I realized my call was not so much a call for service abroad as it was a call for rededication. In fact, my final surrender resulted in no special conviction to work either at home or abroad. To do His will was the thing that counted most.

Since my surrender resulted in a definite desire to do God's will, it was only logical that I should determine His will by prayerfully turning to His Word. I soon discovered that I had already met the first requirement for knowing God's will by presenting my body a living sacrifice:

"I urge you therefore, brethren, by the mercies of God to present your bodies a living and holy sacrifice, acceptable to God, which is your spiritual service of worship. And do not be conformed to this world, but be transformed by the renewing of your mind, that you may prove what the will of God is, that which is good and acceptable and perfect" (Rom. 11:1,2).

The Word was also plain in revealing God's will concerning my place in His vineyard. It was found in the command: "Go ye into all the world and preach the Gospel" (Mark 16:15 KJV). When the Lord said, "GO!", I couldn't interpret that as meaning, "STAY." And I couldn't interpret His, "Go YE," as meaning not me but John Begley or somebody else. When He said, "Go ye into all the WORLD," I couldn't interpret that as meaning, "Go ye into one-third of the world." And not by any far stretch of the imagination could I interpret, "Go ye into all the world and PREACH the Gospel" as meaning "Go ye into all the world and ENJOY the Gospel." Surely if Christ had wanted to qualify His statements He could easily have done it; so, when He said, "Dan Carr, go ye into all the world and preach the Gospel," He meant, "Dan Carr, go ye into all the world and preach the Gospel."

I soon understood that God's vineyard is the WORLD and faced the question of, "Just where in the world would God have me serve?" Should I serve him on a foreign mission field? If so, what constitutes a foreign missionary call?

A number of my friends had a quick answer to this question, "Just wait and pray until you receive the call." In fact, this seemed to be the standard answer in those days. This caused me to believe that the call carried with it some sort of an emotional experience, some sort of a hunch or feeling. It was pointed out to me that Paul received a real foreign missionary call to Macedonia while he was in Troas (Acts 16:9-10); therefore I, too, should wait for such a call. The truth of the matter is that Paul was already on the foreign mission field when he received his call to Macedonia. It was not a call to missionary service but a call to extend his missionary service from Asia to Europe.

Well, I waited and prayed, but "the call" never came. Finally, and only after remembering my own conversion experience, I realized that a call to missionary service didn't necessarily depend upon an emotional experience but rather upon God's simple and direct command: "Go ye into all the world and preach the Gospel."

Other friends of mine told me that the call is a "blanket-call" to all Christians. If this be true, then every Christian should be a missionary. We might as well forget the idea of a "special mission call." There is a certain amount of truth in the idea that all Christians are missionaries. But if carried too far, this thinking can become dangerous. This reminds me of the old Chinese proverb: "If two men feed a horse, the horse will die of starvation." The meaning is that each one will think that the other one has taken the responsibility of feeding the horse. The result is that neither one takes the responsibility and the poor horse dies of starvation.

The same principle applies to Missions. If all Christians are missionaries, then no one really takes the responsibility of getting the Gospel out. It is alright to say that every Christian is a witness, but it is not right to say that every Christian is a missionary.

God's command in Acts 1:8 for us to be witnesses for him throughout the world relates to each one of us personally and privately. It's a direct command for all of us to go and witness. Let's not put the responsibility on others.

It's too bad that the term "missionary call" was ever added to our vocabularies. The call in question is really a call to the MINISTRY OF THE WORD. This is a special call to lifetime service for the Lord and knows no boundaries. It's the same call that the twelve apostles received, and they were determined to carry out that call. We find their testimony in Acts 6:4, "We will devote ourselves to prayer, and to the ministry of the word."

I like the way Ephesians 4:11 spells out the ministry of the Word: "And he gave some as apostles, and some as prophets, and some as evangelists, and some as pastors and teachers." Of course no one has all of these gifts and no one is expected to do the whole ministry. I would soon learn that my gift was that of an evangelist.

This call to the ministry of the Word plus DIRECTION determines our field of service, whether it be at home or abroad. This direction came to me in several ways. First of all, it came through godly parents who steered me in the right direction, through dedicated Christian friends like John Begley who took a personal interest in my spiritual growth, through my pastor who advised me before and during my study for the ministry, through my college roommate who helped me spiritually and encouraged me to read *The Splendor of God* by Honore Morrow, and through missionary acquaintances of mine who talked to me about the possibility of serving as a missionary. One of those missionaries was Virgil Hook of the China Inland Mission. He was a pioneer missionary to Tibet, and his prayer letters caused me to take a real interest in the spiritual need among the tribal people in the mountains of West China. Perhaps I could help meet that need.

God's Word gave me all the direction I needed and as I prayed about a definite field in which to serve, I found comfort in the promise and direction that he gave to Abraham, "The Lord said, 'Go to the land which I will show you.'"

"I SAID, HERE AM I. SEND ME!"

"ME? A MISSIONARY?"

Chapter 3

"THE LORD SAID, 'GO TO THE LAND WHICH I WILL SHOW YOU'"

"The Lord said to Abram, 'Go forth from your country, and from your relatives, and from your father's house, to the land which I will show you.'"
(Genesis 12:1)

I have always been amazed at the way Abraham answered his call to a foreign field. There was no hesitation at all. God said, "GO," and he WENT. This was a good lesson for me. The Lord first showed me the land in which I was to serve by leading me into a survey of His great vineyard. Questions were asked, books were read, courses were taken, missionary contacts were made and prayer was constant. After completing the survey, I found that my interest and attention began to focus on China. It was hard to believe that almost one-third of the unbelievers in the world were to be found in China and that this vast horde was increasing more rapidly by natural propagation than the Christian population was by spiritual propagation. These facts left no question in my mind and heart about the need for laborers in China. It seemed only logical that China was God's place for me.

Up to this point, I had only heard about this great need overseas through the testimonies and writings of those who had or were serving abroad. It was a CRISIS EXPERIENCE that convinced me that God was showing me the land to which I was to go. Even though the door to China was closed when the Japanese attacked Pearl Harbor on December 7, 1941, God always has a way of making good His word. I felt that he would show me that land even though the prospect sounded so unreasonable in the light of a world at war, but show me the land He did. He escorted old Moses to the top of Mount Nebo and showed him the Land of Promise. In my case, I was escorted into the U.S. Navy and shown the land of China.

Finding the door to China closed, I answered the call for Navy chaplains. At the same time, I made another big decision. I proposed to a wonderful and beautiful brown-haired mountain girl whom I had met in seminary. What a joy it was to be united in marriage to her in her home church in Parkersburg, West Virginia, on June 6th, 1943—"D-Day" in Europe. We were also united in a common cause to evangelize the people of China. Lucille had dedicated her life to foreign missionary service when she was just nine years of age.

After serving as a chaplain at the Naval Air Base in Jacksonville, Forida, and also at the Naval Hospital in the same city, I received my orders to join the Seventh Fleet in the South Pacific. This I was anxious to do. Realizing that a number of fellows were facing the possibility of not coming back alive and believing the natural question for them to ask when facing death to be, "What must I do to be saved?", I wanted to be there with the answer to that question: "Believe on the Lord Jesus Christ and thou shalt be saved..." (Acts 16:31 KJV).

It wasn't long before a number of sailors began to ask me that question. We were on a troop ship heading for the Philippines in convoy. They couldn't understand why I was so anxious to get out where the action was, but they just didn't know what was going on in my heart and mind. It wasn't because of any desire on my part to see the horrors of war. God forbid! It was because of a deep conviction that I was called of God to win the lost to Christ, not only our servicemen in the Philippines but also the people of the Orient. At this particular time I was concerned about the men who were with me in that convoy bound for the Orient.

The rule of convoy was that if a ship broke down, the rest of the convoy would continue on without it. It was better to lose one ship than a whole convoy. Well, this is what happened to our ship. As we passed Guam and headed for the Philippines, our ship lost steam and came to a standstill. We were easy prey for Japanese submarines and a disquieting feeling came upon us as the rest of the convoy went on, wishing us good luck.

The enlisted personnel were normally bunked below in "torpedo junction." But in this dangerous situation, many of them rushed topside and slept on deck. I invited some of them to sleep on the floor of my quarters. How surprised I was to find that one of them was a fellow student in Petaluma High School. As I had expected, a number of the sailors hovered around me and asked the question, "What must I do to be saved?" How glad I was to give them the answer to that question.

We were finally able to get up steam and limp along as one American ship was torpedoed just beyond the horizon. What a relief it was to reach the little island of Ulithi. After waiting for the danger to pass, we joined another convoy and continued on our voyage, crossing the spot where the U.S.S. Indianapolis was torpedoed just a few days later, the biggest naval loss in all of World War II.

In due time we reached the Philippines, and I soon found myself serving a bunch of Seabees. A finer bunch of fellows was hard to find. Most of them were older men who had worked at some trade before the war started. It didn't take long to point them to the Divine Carpenter since they themselves were skilled craftsmen and they showed their respect by erecting a chapel and dedicating it to the Master Workman who appeared in a stained glass window in the chapel.

I also had the privilege of turning a number of Filipinos to the same Master and thus received my first taste of foreign missionary work. God blessed my witness among them and also my system of promising chewing gum to any child who would listen attentively to the stories I told about Jesus and His love.

There is one incident I'll never forget. While passing through a country place, I saw a number of men and women working feverishly to gather in an overripe crop while Filipino guerrillas stood guard against possible Japanese attack. It really looked like a life and death struggle, and truly it was for the enemy had consumed most of their foodstuffs and slaughtered their livestock. Yes, everything else was forgotten in the expediency of the task at hand. They thought and spoke and acted solely in terms of the harvest. The only time they relaxed and laughed was when I barged in and helped them in their reaping.

It was this scene that challenged me to work just as earnestly and feverishly over that infinitely more precious harvest of souls about me, ripe for the reaping but doomed to die unless quickly gathered in. I, for one, didn't want to cause the Lord shame by sleeping in His harvest field. "He who gathers in summer is a son who acts wisely, but he who sleeps in harvest is a son who acts shamefully" (Prov. 10:5). So off I went to gather in sailors, soldiers, nationals, and others who came within reaping distance.

My first glimpse of the land to which God had called me was from a Navy Coronado bomber on a patrol hop along the China coast. At the end of the war, my orders took me to the mainland of China where I got a much closer look at the land. Soon after landing in Shanghai, I got my first whiff of the "honey-pots" of China. These carts with iron troughs filled with human waste were pushed by coolies through the streets of the city. They finally spread the contents on their gardens. What more could you want in the way of a potent fertilizer?

My first move in Shanghai was to hop into a ricksha and ask the boy to tow me around the streets on a sight-seeing tour. That fellow passed everything on the road, including trolley cars. Believe it or not, he ran for several miles without changing his pace or stopping for a rest. He wasn't even breathing hard when I begged him to stop and traded places with him. I don't know whether he appreciated it or not, but I sure needed the exercise.

"THE LORD SAID, 'GO TO THE LAND ...'"

My visit to the China Inland Mission compound was the high point of my duty in Shanghai. I was given a royal welcome by missionaries who had just been released from Japanese internment camps and who were recovering from the bad treatment they had received there. Many talks with these missionaries and a firsthand look at the tremendous need in the land sealed my call to China as a missionary.

Yes, my call to China was sealed; but before I could return to China as a missionary, two things had to be accomplished. First of all, I had to complete my duty as a chaplain. Secondly, the Lord would have to lead me to a mission board and take care of the matter of my "being recommended by the brethren."

"ME? A MISSIONARY?"

Chapter 4

"BEING RECOMMENDED BY THE BRETHREN"

"And Paul chose Silas, and departed, being recommended by the brethren unto the grace of God." (Acts 15:40 KJV)

A man might feel called to the mission field and meet all the requirements; but, unless he be recommended and appointed by the brethren at home, his chances for reaching the field and doing an effective piece of work are slim. The Holy Spirit is ever constraining the ministers of our churches to separate His chosen vessels for the work to which He has called them. Such was the case with Paul and Silas. After being recommended by the brethren, they went through Syria and Cilicia, confirming the churches.

I was still in the Philippines when word came to me from Dr. Lewis J. Julianel, pastor of my home church in San Francisco, that the Conservative Baptist Foreign Mission Society was ready to start work in India and Africa, and I found myself beseeching the Lord to include China on the society's list of prospective fields. But China was so big. Even if the Lord should lay it on the hearts of the board members to open a work in China, would that insure work among the tribes on the western border?

Well, believing that action goes right along with prayer, I decided to write the society and find out its attitude towards China. Back came the answer in August 1945: "We are now praying that God will undertake in the border section of West China where one of our appointees is investigating while serving in the U.S. Army." This encouraging report from Dr. Ray Buker, the Foreign Secretary, quickened my faith and I continued to pray until another report from Dr. Buker arrived in December of the same year: "An appointee has worked out a field in West China where we will be doing pioneer work. It seems to fit exactly the call of the Holy Spirit in your heart."

My cup was full and overflowing, and I wasted no time in submitting my application. And again I went back to the business of prayer until this word came through: "Prospects appear bright for a good start in West China. The rest depends upon us as members of the mission and on our dependence on God in the planning and execution of the great task ahead." And then, in January 1946, the following notice arrived: "This is to officially acknowledge the receipt of your application. We can't tell you how happy we are to feel that you will soon possibly be a member of our mission family."

My term of service as a chaplain ended with my being evacuated to the States as the result of an injury sustained in the Islands. And those seven months that I spent in naval hospitals in the Philippines and the United States were months of blessing, for God used them to prepare me spiritually for the work ahead of carrying His message to China.

I was well aware of the fact that only the Lord could prepare me spiritually for the task that was ahead, but I was of the opinion that I would have to help the Lord when it came to the matter of temporal things. Certainly this was my opinion, not the Lord's. I thought I would have to do something to insure our travel on the field. I had read that no trains were available to transport us to our field of work on the Tibetan border. Furthermore, the washboard motor roads were controlled by bandits. It seemed to me that these problems could be overcome if we had the use of a little plane on the field, and what better man was there to fly that plane than Dan Carr.

Since I had plenty of spare time while convalescing at the Naval Hospital in Philadelphia, I made my way out to the Flying Dutchman Airport in Somerton, Pennsylvania. One of the first people I met there was a young fellow by the name of "Kelley" (Nate) Saint who was building up flight time. He was a very humble and dedicated Christian and was looking forward to serving in the jungles of Ecuador under the Missionary Aviation Fellowship as a missionary pilot and mechanic. What a wonderful time we had together sharing our missionary callings. I was impressed by his complete dedication and determination to reach his missionary goal. What a blessing I received as he prayed for me and encouraged me to press on to my goal of carrying the Gospel message to the people living on China's western border. How shocked I was ten years later when the word came to us in Taiwan that "Kelley" Saint and four of his fellow missionaries had flown into the jungles and suffered

"BEING RECOMMENDED BY THE BRETHREN" 27

martyrdom at the hands of the Auca Indians they were trying to reach for Christ.

I must confess that "Kelley" questioned my flying small single-engine planes near the "roof" of the world and finding suitable repair facilities in such an out-of-the-way part of the world, but that didn't deter me from my goal of securing a pilot's license. My instructor had been a fighter pilot during the war and wasn't too impressed by this chaplain who wanted to become a pilot, but he was very kind and patient as he supervised the feeble efforts of this man with a cross on his collar. What a relief it was to him when I finally received my license to fly.

I'm sure he looked back at the many times I caused his hair to stand on end. For instance, there was the time I decided to go up and practice some stalls and tailspins. I was flying a Piper Cub. Right in the middle of a spin the prop stopped. I frantically looked for a place to land. The best place seemed to be a field filled with haystacks. I lined the plane up between two rows of stacks and made a perfect three-point landing, clipping off the tops of the stacks on both sides of me. In no time at all, I scrambled out of the plane and fell flat on the ground. My legs just wouldn't hold me up. They were trembling like a leaf. Up to this time I hadn't had time to be frightened. There was too much to do, and that included praying.

Adding to my misery was the gathering of a number of farmers around me, all scolding me for flying over their land everyday and spooking their cattle. The fact of the matter was that this was the first time I had ever flown over their land. I quickly apologized for scaring their cattle that day but not for doing the same on other days. At first they didn't believe me because they had looked up at the letters and numbers on the plane flying over them each day and noticed that the numbers were always the same. They didn't realize that all of the yellow cub planes flying over them everyday had the same letters and numbers except for the last number. That last number on a plane distinguished it from the other planes. These farmers had noticed most of the numbers and thought they were all the same. My explanation plus the cross on my collar finally convinced them that I was telling the truth. Some were a little uneasy when I gave the Lord all the credit for helping me make a safe landing and that He could help them make a safe landing in Heaven.

"ME? A MISSIONARY?"

They did a good job of taking down fences and helping me push the plane into a clear field. One of them led me over to his farmhouse and let me use his telephone to call the Flying Dutchman Airport. The regulation was that any student pilot making a forced landing was not allowed to fly the plane out himself. That was the job of the instructor. My instructor arrived about an hour later in a jeep. I knew what he was thinking when he walked up to me, "Chaplain, how did you ever make a safe landing?"

Since I had not yet learned how to spin a prop, he told me to get into the plane and handle the switch to the motor while he spun the prop. He yelled, "Switch off!" as he prepared to prime the engine. I yelled right back, "Switch off!" just as I had done everytime I had made ready to fly a plane. He turned the prop, the engine caught, and he went flying head over heals into the dust. It's a wonder he came out alive. What had happened? I had forgotten to turn off the switch when I had made that emergency landing.

That poor instructor had every right to bawl me out for my stupidity, but he held his peace. One thing he did do, however, was to say, "Chaplain, when I yell, 'Switch off!' make sure the switch is off." After priming the engine, he yelled, "Switch on!" I turned on the switch. He spun the prop. The engine caught. I climbed out of the plane. He climbed in and flew the plane back to the airport while I drove the jeep back to the same place, dripping with sweat and suffering complete embarrassment.

What did I learn from all my training at the Flying Dutchman Airport? I learned that "Kelley" Saint was right about the problem of flying a small plane on the border of Tibet. The idea was ridiculous. I would have had to make a roundtrip flight of 1,000 miles to buy aviation gasoline and have repairs made on the plane. What if the plane couldn't fly in the first place?

The most important thing I learned from all of this was that I should ask the Lord to make His will known in all temporal matters as well as spiritual matters. This included my remaining months of treatment at the hospital.

My morale was really boosted when Lucille arrived at the hospital with the heir to the fortune which I did not have. Dan, Jr., had made his debut while I was still overseas, and this was my first chance to see him. Our happy reunion was made doubly happy when the good news arrived that our preliminary applications to the mission board had been looked upon with favor. There was also a request for us to appear before the Candidate Committee. A few months later I was out of the hospital and standing before that committee with fear and great trembling, but the expected ordeal wasn't an ordeal afterall. In fact, it was a time of inspiration and encouragement for this missionary-to-be. The members of the committee lent a sympathetic ear to my word of testimony and were extremely kind yet firm in their questioning of my doctrinal beliefs.

The next day found me giving my testimony to the entire mission board and being welcomed into the mission family. And a happy family it was as the members lifted their voices in prayer and thanksgiving for those who had just been recommended for service abroad. This was an experience never to be forgotten, and those tears of rejoicing will linger forever in my memories.

Things reached a climax at the Commissioning Service. One of the board members had this to say about that service:

> *The new missionary appointees entered the auditorium carrying flags of the countries to which they were going and stood in the formation of a "V" while they sang, "We've a Savior to show to the nations." They responded to the roll call with three-minute testimonies telling why they wanted to heed the call of the Master to go to sin-darkened people. It*

30   "ME? A MISSIONARY?"

was a time of rededication for all present when we stood to our feet with moist eyes, singing, "Give of thy sons to bear the message glorious" and pledged ourselves to stand behind this splendid group with our prayers.

Several months of deputation work were followed by days of routine preparation: the securing of passports and necessary visas, the securing of many items of clothing and equipment, the final physical examination, and the securing of the medical report with recommendations for us to follow on the field. Worst of all were the innoculations that we had to receive to satisfy the requirements of the Chinese government and to safeguard our health in the land of China.

Our final act before sailing was to join the rest of our missionaries in a series of farewell services along the west coast of the United States. My biggest thrill was the send-off given us by the members of my home church, the First Baptist Church of San

"BEING RECOMMENDED BY THE BRETHREN"

Francisco. These were the folk who had licensed me to preach some ten years before and had followed me all the way with their prayers.

These services brought to a close the many months of preparation. At the final service, the General Director of our Conservative Baptist Foreign Mission Society, Dr. Vincent Brushwyler, gave a summary of those months:

> *During these months of preparation, the anticipation of the great experience in the lands beyond become more and more keen. And finally will come the day of embarkation! There will be farewells, tears, and perhaps a little heartache. But the curtain that closes the period of preparation and anticipation will open a new and glorious era of realization and occupation. There will be a song of joy in the heart, though expressed through lips that quiver and revealed by a countenance that is tear-stained! The real missionary experience has begun!*

This missionary experience began for me and my family on December 15, 1946, when we were given a final farewell by our friends and relatives "and accompanied unto the ship."

Chapter 5

"AND ACCOMPANIED UNTO THE SHIP"

"And they all wept much, and fell on Paul's neck, and kissed him, sorrowing most of all for the words which he spoke, that they should see his face no more. And they accompanied him unto the ship."
(Acts 20:38 NKJV)

As Paul said farewell to the Ephesian elders in Miletus, he must have known in his heart that he would never see them again. The Holy Spirit was leading him back to Jerusalem where he would suffer great persecution and imprisonment. Certainly the brethren must have detected what was going on in Paul's heart as they expressed their Christian love by kissing him and accompanying him to the ship that would take him on the first leg of his journey to martyrdom.

Even though we had no thought of martyrdom, we had similar feelings as we made ready to say goodbye to our friends and loved ones and set sail for China. Some of them even expressed fear that they would never see us again. As for us missionaries, we did shed some tears and experience heartache as Dr. Brushwyler had predicted, but the joy and anticipation of carrying the Gospel to China far out-weighed the sadness.

Week after week we had sought to carry out our sailing orders, but a maritime strike had tied up all shipping along the west coast. Sailing dates were repeatedly postponed. That familiar notice "Just a word to let you know that the sailing of the *Marine Lynx* has been postponed" provided the framework for many a joke. Our ship's uncanny ability to miss all sailing dates resulted in its being nicknamed the evolutionary "Missing Link." And certainly it was the "missing link" in our passage to China.

Through the courtesy of the American President Lines, this special missionary ship had been fitted and was ready to carry several hundred missionaries to the Orient. But this willingness to help on the part of the shipowners found no counterpart in those who manned the ship. Their demand for higher wages was far more important to them than the shipping out of missionaries. It was right at this point that we had to heed the scriptural injunction to "be patient toward all men," even longshoremen and those who manned the ships. Our patience was finally rewarded with a sudden break in the strike, a break which lasted just long enough for us to board our ship and sail.

Patience also brought to the world's attention our field of labor in West China. Shortly before sailing from San Francisco, the local newspapers head-lined the possibility of American airmen crashing in flights "over the hump" during World War II and being taken as slaves by fierce Nosu tribesmen, more commonly called "Lolos." This was the report that a Catholic priest had given to American officials. He claimed that he had seen some Americans held captive by the Nosu.

At that time it was estimated that there were a million and a half Nosu living in the mountainous area of southern Xikang Province, and these were the people we expected to reach for Christ. They are of Burmo-Tibetan origin and not related to the Chinese. Centuries ago the Chinese, the Han people, entered the tribal areas on the border of West China. They drove the tribal people up into the barren mountains and took the fertile valleys for themselves—similar to what white Americans did to Indian Americans during their conquest of the West. Because of this, a real hatred existed between the Nosu and the Chinese.

U.S. Army search and rescue teams had entered Nosuland, hoping to ransom any flyers that might have been taken captive, but they were unsuccessful. These mountain people had a reputation for collecting ransom for Chinese they had taken captive. The towns and villages in the area were surrounded by high walls, for these tribespeople would often raid the villages and carry off Chinese as slaves. Even before leaving the States, we were praying that God might open up the doorway to the hearts of these people.

Finally, on the morning of December 15, 1946, our friends and loved ones and several of our mission leaders accompanied our little party of Conservative Baptist missionaries to the ship and saw us safely aboard. The other members of this missionary party were to play a central role in much of this story and, certainly, in our lives.

The senior missionaries in this party were Lee and Ida Lovegren. They had served a number of years in China and were now ready to lead us in the opening of a pioneer work in West

China. Next in seniority was Ruth Mayo, a registered nurse, and scheduled to do orphanage work in South China. She was to be assisted by Bennie and Dorothy Benson upon the completion of their language study in Chengdu. Then there was John and Irene Simpson with their little daughter, Lynn Ann. John had already seen several years of missionary work among the Lisu tribespeople in Yunnan Province. His wife, a registered nurse, was ready to give a major portion of her time to our proposed medical work. The only single male member of our party was Ralph Covell, a fellow classmate of ours in seminary and destined to become our closest associate in the work. Especially gifted in linguistics, he was to give a portion of his time to Bible translation work among the tribes.

These were the folk who would share with us in the work—educators, nurses, linguists, evangelists, yet missionaries all. Each was to make a valuable contribution to the work as a whole. What a thrill it was to stand with them on the deck of that long-awaited ship and look out over the crowd which had gathered to bid Godspeed to the largest party of missionaries ever to sail from America—over 400 of them, plus their children.

What a joy it was to be numbered among that missionary band! And what a challenge it was to our hearts as the crowd joined us in singing, "Publish glad tidings, tidings of peace, tidings of Jesus, redemption and release." But in the midst of all this singing, I suddenly remembered that I had left my passport in a luggage shop near the dock. How in the world could I publish glad tidings in China if I didn't have a passport to get into the country?

I must have broken all records racing down the gangplank and scooting along the dock to that shop. Apparently the proprietor was expecting me, for he already had my passport in his hand as he shouted, "Welcome back! I kind of thought you'd be needing this!" It didn't take me long to thank him and fly back to the ship. The captain was on the bridge shouting, "All aboard!" The crew was getting ready to hoist the gangplank. My wife was leaning over the rail looking for her lost husband. My son was crying in her arms. The crowd was cheering as I grabbed the gangplank. And I was exhausted as I climbed aboard.

After regaining my breath and composure, I joined the other missionaries as they lined up along the rail and waved to the crowd. How strengthening it was to glimpse among that great sea of faces many whose prayers we knew would follow us. What a comfort to know that "though sundered far," we could still meet with them "around that common Mercy Seat!"

What a glorious send-off, yet what a sinking feeling as first the people and then the land faded from my view. I could appreciate the feeling Paul must have had as he said "goodbye" to the Ephesian elders. But that sinking feeling soon gave way to an anxious anticipation of what lay ahead, even wondering about the Bible's comment on "the way of a ship in the midst of the sea." I had never really paused to consider "the way of a ship in the midst of the sea" until that day we sailed out through the Golden Gate. Our mission society had given us this advance warning about our particular ship:

> *Through the cooperation of the American President Lines, it is possible for you to be on your way to the field to which the Lord has called you who might otherwise be still waiting around for transportation. You will find conditions on the ship on which you are to sail considerably different from those of passenger ships before the war. You will be subjected to certain inconveniences due to the fact that it is a troop ship and has not yet been converted to passenger service. You have chosen to submit to these inconveniences because you are eager to be at your work. You can say with missionary Paul, "Therefore I endure everything for the sake of the elect, that they too may obtain the salvation that is in Christ Jesus, with eternal glory" (2 Tim. 2:10).*

Well, that was the warning given us by our mission society. A final word of warning came from the shipping company:

> *Again we feel that we must call to your attention the fact that the space available is not first class. In order that there may be no misunderstanding, we outline briefly the conditions under which these bookings must be made: (1) Accommodations will be in Emergency Class Hatches (no portholes) 2,3,4,5,6 and will consist of three or four high bunks of which approximately 60% will be utilized for sleeping and the balance as baggage racks; (2) Passengers must keep their own sleeping quarters clean and must make their own beds; (3) Food will be served "cafeteria" style.*

Even though we didn't relish the idea of being crowded in the hold of a ship with several hundred other missionaries, we rather enjoyed the ordeal. The women and children were assigned to hatches set aside for them. The men were placed in other hatches. During the daylight hours they could get together. This gave us a wonderful time to chat with those of kindred mind and calling. Those hours and days of blessed fellowship far out-weighed any and all of the physical discomforts that were ours.

The voyage across the alleged "peaceful" Pacific Ocean was very interesting for about three days—that is, three days after the first two days of "wishing you were dead" seasickness. After that, it was little more than a lot of water. I can best describe it in the words of that old song: "I joined the Navy to see the sea. What did I see? I saw the sea." And sometimes that sea was so rough that it caused the loss of a goodly number of appetites plus equally as many meals. I'll never forget the number of times I boldly started down that chow line only to drop out at the sight and smell of food. And to think that I was an "old salt" just out of the Navy. What a jolt it was to my pride to have my companions, even my wife, laugh at me in my misery.

Having finally gotten my "sea legs again," I began to enjoy the trip. Christmas was especially memorable. There was a Christmas tree with all the trimmings and even Santa made his appearance and distributed gifts to all of the children. It was with happy hearts that we all joined together in singing carols and paying special homage to the One who had led us thus far.

A Chinese fortune teller would have offered the mole on my right eyebrow as sure proof that fate had led me thus far; but in my heart, I knew it was the Lord. After fifteen days of His safe leading and the loss of Ralph Covell's birthday because of the International Date Line, "I came into Asia."

Chapter 6

"I CAME INTO ASIA"

"And when they were come to him, he said unto them, 'Ye know, from the first day that I came into Asia, after what manner I have been with you at all seasons'." (Acts 20:18 KJV)

Paul was well up on his seasons when he came into Asia, and so was I when I entered Asia almost 2,000 years later. It was early Tuesday morning, December 31, 1946, the day before New Years, that our ship entered the mouth of the mighty Yangtze River, gateway to the oldest of Asia's existing nations, CHINA!

Incidentally, the Chinese do not attach the name "China" to their country, nor have they ever done so in the past. "China" is simply a word used by foreigners to designate that land which has long been known to its own people as "Jung-Guo" or "The Middle Kingdom." The term "Middle Kingdom" came into popular use early in China's feudal age and was based on a Confucian belief that Heaven was round and that China occupied the central spot in a four-square world. It was visualized as a superior domain surrounded by uncouth barbarians.

One of the first references to this name can be found in a poem taken from the ancient *Book of Odes* in which the Emperor Li is admonished in the following words: "And still you and your creatures go on in this course. Indignation is rife against you here in the Middle Kingdom and extends to the demon regions." After leaving one of those "demon regions," the United States, we had finally arrived in the "Middle Kingdom."

After steaming fifty miles up China's main artery, the Yangtze River, we swung hard aport and followed the tide up a tributary, the Huangpu River, to Shanghai. Commercial and naval craft from many nations were to be seen on every side. And clumsy junks and deftly sculled sampans swarmed about us as we edged our way into this teaming metropolis of some 5,000,000 people.

As we disembarked and made our way through the streets of Shanghai, we were impressed by the number of people milling about us. With a little persuasion, I could easily have believed that all of China's millions were to be found in Shanghai. People! People everywhere! Just where did they all come from?

One answer to this question of population might be taken right out of Chinese history. It seems as though "mass production" on the part of the Chinese started back in 494 B.C. when the King of Yue, ruler of the Zhejiang area, was taken captive by the King of Wu, who controlled the Jiangsu area. Upon his release and restoration to his own throne, he began making plans to wreak revenge. Chief among his plans was the order for an increase in the population. Due to the war, his domain was sadly lacking in manpower. New "cannon-fodder" was needed. Ignoring the moral code, the King of Yue encouraged the remarrying of widows and widowers and punished the parents of any daughter or son not married by the age of seventeen or twenty, respectively. Imprisonment, fines, and other forms of punishment were heaped upon the parents until their eligible offspring were married. He even went so far as to offer a bonus for any new addition to the population. And as might be expected, old women were not to be married, not even for their wealth; and old men were not allowed to claim young wives.

This "mass production" plan finally resulted in the overthrow and suicide of the King of Wu and in the establishment of a new custom of marrying young. Attempts were made by later rulers to stamp out the practice; but its influence was to remain long in the land, even to the day we drove through that milling throng on the streets of Shanghai.

The streets of Shanghai provided another spectacle. How our bus driver managed to weave his way through them is a mystery still to be solved. I was always under the impression that a motorist had at least a theoretical responsibility toward other drivers and to pedestrians. This was not true in Shanghai. From my vantage point in the rear, I could see our driver shove the accelerator into the floorboards, lean on the horn, and simply burst through traffic like a bull in a china closet, counting on his horn to get him the right of way at intersections.

Although most of my time was spent in back-seat driving with every muscle in my body, I did manage to catch a glimpse of the city. To say that Shanghai is representative of China is to misinterpret the facts. Actually, it is a fantastic mixture of both Occident and Orient. Here they meet, clash in some things, merge in others and yet are reluctant to bow to each other. Trolleys and buses jammed with people rush through the streets, noisily clanging and honking at the much slower mass of pedestrians, bicycles, rickshas, and pedicabs (a tri-wheeled bike and cab contraption). Large edifices seemingly plucked from the Occident cast their shadows over the traditional Chinese dwellings; and stores, featuring the latest in Parisian fashions, "rub elbows" with the shops of old China. Clumsy junks share the water with giant steamers.

"ME? A MISSIONARY?"

We arrived in China with the Occident's mania for speed; but here we were to learn, although not unwillingly, the old Chinese proverb: "You yourself are urgent about the matter, but others are in no hurry." Chinese motorists are the one exception to the proverb.

Thanks to the help of the China Christian Council, we were able to find lodging in the old French Quarter of the city with the Ralph Mortensons of the China Bible Society. We soon learned the meaning of the old Chinese saying, "make haste slowly," as one thing after another impeded our progress. First, the baggage and freight had to pass through what was sometimes called the world's worst customs' house. Although we haunted the place with our presence, no one was impressed with the urgency of our mission.

Customs might not have been impressed with our mission, but we certainly were impressed with theirs when they finally mustered enough time to examine our things. One little bribe passed under a table would have turned away our tide of difficulties; but, "for conscience sake," we were forced to "render customs to whom customs is due." Consequently, we were charged for things we did not have and not charged for things we had.

One member of our party, Bennie Benson, made the unfortunate mistake of calling the customs inspector's attention to the fact that he had been charged for two typewriters when he only had one. The inspector's reply was, "Oh, I'm very sorry, Mr. Benson. I'll tell you what I'll do. I'll examine your things again," and so he did. The outcome was a far more thorough examination of his freight which scratched the second typewriter fee but added a new list of additional fees on things which had been overlooked in the first examination. As could be expected, the latter charge was far greater than the first. Bennie's unfortunate experience, plus numerous blunders on the part of his associates, caused him to make a classic remark which later found double-duty on the tongues of all of us: "The trouble with us missionaries is that we think too much."

Added to our difficulty of "thinking too much" was the advent of Chinese New Year. It began on the twenty third day of the Twelfth Moon of the lunar year, on the very night that the God of the Kitchen is given a royal send-off to Paradise after a year's service in the world. The following days were spent in preparing for this return on the first day of the new year. Such preparation called for plenty of red paper, incense sticks and plenty of foodstuffs since stores and offices are closed on New Years Day and often remain closed for the duration of the festivities which usually last about two weeks.

What perturbed us most at this particular time was the realization that we had to play second fiddle to an old kitchen god. The biggest portion of our business was left undone since most of the firms were closed and since work done during this season required a big tip for services rendered. A better word would be "bribe."

While the "Better Half" and I spent New Year's eve reading under a little, forty watt light bulb, Chinese families were spending it in comparative darkness. The only light burning in their homes was a big, red candle. Ushering in the new year by candlelight is supposed to insure good luck for all.

As the door of each house is opened on New Year's morn, a bombardment of firecrackers is set off to chase away any evil spirits that might be lurking on the outside. This is followed by the father and favorite son or some other member of the family starting off by foot or vehicle to welcome the God of Happiness. The direction changes with the coming of each new year. Consequently, an almanac must be consulted to ward off the possibility of welcoming the wrong god.

Having frightened away the spirits, and having welcomed the God of Happiness, the family conducts a worship service in which due respect is paid to its ancestors, and sacrifices are made to the Kitchen God who supposedly returns from Paradise on that day. The service ends with the children kneeling and offering the season's greeting to their parents.

After four days of entertainment and amusement, the God of Wealth is welcomed. Although he takes his annual leave on New Year's eve, no attention is paid him until the eve of the fourth day when he returns from Paradise. His departure is never celebrated since it is a bad omen to bid farewell to the God of Wealth.

Following hard on the heels of the "God of Wealth Day" comes the "Lantern Festival" which starts on the eighteenth day of the First Moon and ending a week later with the actual festival, thus bringing to a close the prolonged New Year's celebration. During this period, lamps of every size and description are displayed on the streets with only red candles being used on the inside of the lanterns. The use of white or green candles would spell bad luck since white and green symbolize death, melancholy, and misfortune.

I may have used a white candle on the evening of the Lantern Festival or my right ear may have hummed around 11:00 o'clock; but in either case, I was to meet misfortune the very next day. Most Chinese would probably have favored the latter suggestion since such a humming in one's right ear at that particular time is a sure sign that he will lose money.

It all happened at a bus stop on the corner of Edward II Avenue and the Bund, a large boulevard which runs along the water front. I had finished my business in town and was putting in my bid for a Frenchtown bus. Several hundred of us were bunched along the pavement waiting for a good, old "Number 22" bus. A few moments later it pulled in and discharged all but one passenger. That lone survivor tried his best to leave. But a swarm of humanity, trying to enter the one single door of the bus at the same time, proved a little too much for him.

I had reached the doorway first and could have entered, but my brief case was caught between two fellows standing behind me. Had it not been for the crowd pressing on all sides they could have separated a little and freed the thing. Try as I would, I just couldn't drag it into the bus and not wanting to lose my passport and other valuables inside the case, I hung on for dear life. In the meantime, our lone survivor was kicking my face and crawling all over me in his effort to get out. He did manage to get out by rolling over a number of heads. I still remember the fear in his eyes and scream on his lips as he went sailing out over the top of that crowd.

I was still blocking the bus entrance when I struck on a brilliant idea. Since there was no way of pushing those two men back, I finally decided on pushing them up. In a moment, I was between their legs and lifting them bodily into the air. Both of them went up and over my head and into the bus. For some reason or another they had enjoyed their little flight and showed their appreciation by hauling me into the bus after them. Why they even went so far as to wish me a happy "Kung Hsi Fa Tsai," the Chinese equivalent of "Happy New Year."

It was not until I had left the bus and found my wallet missing from my left rear pocket that I realized the irony behind the greeting of those two rascals. It literally means, "I humbly wish you a happy new year and that you become more wealthy." But I soon found comfort in an old Chinese maxim: "If you are lucky, you suffer in pocket; if you are unlucky, you will suffer in person." Afterall, I hadn't lost my life; I had merely lost a hundred American dollars. The wallet with my Navy Identification Card was miraculously returned to me through the agency of the United States Naval Attache. Needless to say, my wallet was confined to inner pockets from that moment on.

It wasn't enough for me to lose a hundred dollars. It was also necessary for me to learn the meaning of "losing one's face." One day I asked a pedicab man who could speak a little English to pedal me to a certain office. Confident that the turning over of my fare had settled my account with him, I left his cab and spent an hour transacting some business.

When I returned to the street, I found myself being hailed by the same pedicab man. Giving him the cold shoulder, I started walking down the street, but he pedaled alongside of me and demanded that I pay him for an hour's wait. Not having told him to wait, I continued to ignore him. When he persisted in tagging along after me, I decided to have some fun. After walking down the busy street for about a hundred yards, I would turn quickly and retrace my steps. I did this a number of times, much to the disgust of the driver who had a terrible time making "U" turns on the busy thoroughfare; but he was intent on collecting that extra money and nothing could throw him off my trail.

Suddenly realizing that my antics were being frowned upon by fellow pedestrians, I changed my tactics and tried to elude my pursuer by running down a little side street, but what I thought was a through street turned out to be a dead-end one. By this time, the driver and other cab drivers with tools in their hands were coming down the street. The driver in question was wielding the seat of his pedicab. One look at his face was enough to convince me that not even the payment of that extra money could save me from a real beating.

With a locked gate in front of me and compound walls on either side of me, there was only one thing left to do. Thrusting a hand into my right coat pocket and making it appear as though I were fingering a gun and trying to cover up my fear, I turned and faced the foe. Fortunately for me, the ruse worked. Backing them up against one of the walls, I made my way past them and held them at bay until I reached the main street. Then throwing caution to the wind, I broke into a run and tried to lose them in the crowd. But two policemen with drawn clubs closed in on me and escorted me back to the scene of the "crime."

After threatening to lock me up and searching me for a hidden weapon in the presence of my pursuers and a crowd of people, they gave me a long lecture in broken English on the Chinese custom of informing pedicab drivers when their services were no longer needed. Furthermore, I was forced to pay my driver at least ten times more than was his due. With "face" completely lost, I ran off like a dog with its tail between its legs while the people jeered. And to think that I could have saved my "face" by paying that extra debt of about eight American cents. Why, I could even have saved the eight cents had my wife been with me on this business trip. She would have ordered me to pay the man.

Along with the loss of my "face" and one hundred dollars was the loss of my appendix. I had spent a busy day squaring away my freight and was in the process of returning home with a duffle bag on my back when I suddenly felt a cramp in my right side. A young missionary walking at my side noticed me slowing down and offered to help me. But an older missionary insisted that fledgling missionaries had to learn, as he had learned many years before, to bear their own burdens. So, on I went carrying my own load and ending up in bed with an acute attack of appendicitis.

My host finally located a bed for me in the Country Hospital and called an ambulance. I thought to myself, "Why couldn't it be a city hospital instead of a country one?" I fully expected the Country Hospital to be some old barn far out on the edge of town.

In fact, I was convinced of this fact when four rough-looking characters, reeking with liquor and garlic, dumped me onto a stretcher as Lucille hovered over me with a look of distress on her face. Then they threw a dirty blanket over my face and lifted me into what was once an old American military ambulance long overdue at the scrap heap.

A rickety ride across town brought me to my destination. I was still perspiring in my blanket when I heard a startled cry: "What are you trying to do, smother the patient? Remove that blanket from his face and be quick about it!" Once out from under that blanket, I found myself staring into the face of a trim, middle-aged English nurse, the matron of the hospital. One look at her concerned face and clean white uniform assured me that I was at least in friendly hands. And a look at my surroundings—marble floors, elevators, foreign doctors in the corridor—left no doubt in my mind that I was also in reliable hands. I soon learned that the Country Hospital was actually the finest hospital in China and located in one of Shanghai's better residential districts. At one time it had been located in the country, but the ever-expanding city had swallowed it up.

I lived the "life of Reilly" during those twelve days in the hospital and found that it catered to foreigners—soft bed, warm room, excellent treatment—and I even talked the head nurse into bringing me extra helpings of food. And best of all was my first bath since leaving the *Marine Lynx*. Only once was I really worried and that was when I weighed myself on the hospital scale. I knew that I must have lost some weight, but when the needle of the scales settled down at 90 my reaction almost ripped my incision wide open. A fellow patient soon quieted my nerves by explaining that the scale registered in kilos, one kilo equalling 2.2 pounds. What a relief it was to learn that I had only lost 14 pounds instead of 122.

My only complaint after a wonderful rest in the Country Hospital was that my witnessing for Christ produced very little in the way of results. My doctor was a medical missionary from the States. My four English-speaking Chinese nurses were all Christians and had taken their training in mission hospitals. One was the daughter of a Methodist minister. Another was a product of the China Inland Mission. The night nurse, a Jewish woman from Jerusalem, turned out to be an ardent atheist and gave no ear to the Gospel message.

"I CAME INTO ASIA"

Lucille and Lee Lovegren escorted me back to our compound on discharge day. Unfortunately, they brought along a pair of Ralph Covell's trousers for me to wear, but Lee's trench coat remedied the situation by hiding the six-inch gap in front. Somehow Ralph and I had gotten our laundry mixed. I was to learn later that he had had similar difficulties on the Yangtze with a pair of my trousers, but his difficulties only involved the making of pleats around the waist.

Once out of the hospital and back on the street again, I found that the whole monetary system had changed, not an unusual occurrence in China. I first discovered this fact when I met with a rebuff at what used to be a private money exchange shop. The owner made me feel like "Public Enemy Number One" when he ordered me off the premises and threatened to call the police if I didn't clear out. Just a month before I had been one of his best customers since I was our mission treasurer and exchanged all American currency for our missionaries.

Private exchange shops had been doing a flourishing business in the open market before the new change-over. Government officials, civilians, and mission societies alike had been using the open market since rates on that market were 100% higher than the official rate of 3,370 Chinese dollars to one American dollar. American currency was actually a commodity being bought at one price and sold at another. New greenbacks were worth more than old ones. Ten and twenty dollar bills brought a higher rate of exchange than bills of lower or higher denomination.

Moving from one exchange shop to another, I was able at times to get as high as 7,000 to 1. I had confined all of my exchange dealings to such shops after having suffered at the hands of street hawkers who short-changed me on more than one occasion. I also had the great misfortune of mistaking a pimp for a hawker. The fellow edged up to me and made some motions similar to those of a professional money hawker. Expecting a good rate of exchange at the end of our trek, I followed the fellow through one dark alley after another and up three flights of rickety stairs only to flee in horror when I found that I had walked right into a house of ill fame.

You can imagine how I felt when the pimp pointed his finger at a room full of prostitutes and asked me, "Which one would you like?"

A juggling of the financial set-up while I was still on the sick list had caused the terms "open market" and "black market" to become synonymous. Perhaps the old open market should rightfully have been called the "open white-black market." The government ordered the closing of all private exchange shops and appointed its own brokers, but the new ruling was short-lived. Those in authority couldn't summon enough power to enforce the order, so things reverted back to normal and the old black market began to flourish again despite the jailing of a few hawkers here and there. Two years later we were to see the rate soar to 350,000,000 Chinese dollars to one American dollar. I would be using a bushel basket filled with millions of Chinese dollars to buy a dozen bananas.

"I CAME INTO ASIA" 51

My little white candle must have burned long on the evening of the Lantern Festival for, added to the riddle of exchange, there were other problems which caused a much longer delay in Shanghai than we had anticipated. But God in his wisdom saw fit to use that delay as a means of introducing us to the Orient gradually.

Although tainted by the Occident, Shanghai still possessed an oriental flavor. Much of the city was definitely "Chinesey" and it was fun meandering along the streets—dirty, yet colorful; junky, yet picturesque—and staring more than enough to be branded as new arrivals.

Since the Chinese virtually live in the streets, we had a wonderful opportunity to watch them. The streets were filled with children who were well-padded against the winter's chill and looking deceivingly fat, children who delighted in calling out "hello" to foreigners. They made us wish so very much that we could tell them of the One who loves children, and they heightened our eagerness to begin language study. Yet, as we walked on past coolies who still act as beasts of burden, past laborers using the slow and simple methods of generations past, and past tea shops where people slowly sip their tea, we were reminded again that in the Orient we would have to learn to be very patient.

Portable street lunch counters offered passersby bowls of rice, noodles, meat cakes, and other national dishes. The pervasive noise of the marketplace teeming with merchants and peddlers introduced to us the seemingly obligatory oriental ritual accompanying any business transaction—choreographed bargaining.

The temples and home altars were a pervasive presence throughout the streets, alleys, and labyrinthine courtyards of this strange land. Though one could admire, perhaps, from a distant objectivity, the artistry of some of the temples, we could only feel the most suffocatingly oppresive grimness and sense of darkness cast across the lives of these multitudes by the ever-present shrines. Even the ever-burning candles didn't seem to cast any light. Truly, "it is a land of idols."

Chapter 7

"IT IS A LAND OF IDOLS"

"It is a land of idols, and they are mad over fearsome idols." (Jer. 50:38)

As we rambled from one temple to another, we couldn't help but remember Jeremiah's comments on the people of Babylon and their ardent worship of idols. He detailed clearly the destruction that would come upon them because of their sins. Not even their idols would be able to save them. We had similar thoughts about the people of China who looked to their idols for salvation. Destruction would finally come upon them despite their ardent idol worship. How anxious we were to point them to the one True God.

Our senior missionaries taught us quite a bit about Chinese religious life. We learned that an ordinary Chinese person is approximately 70% Buddhist and 30% Taoist. This greater influence on the part of Buddhism is probably due to the person's better understanding of the Buddhist writings and greater interest in the Buddhist account of Hell. Underlying his religious belief is a Confucian philosophy of life based on such cardinal virtues as filial piety, benevolence, justice, propriety, intelligence and fidelity.

The Chinese consider Buddhism, Taoism, and Confucianism as being three in one, each complementing the other and attempting to meet a different want in human nature: (1) Confucianism appeals to morality and conduct; (2) Taoism is materialistic; and (3) Buddhism is metaphysical. Whichever God is worshipped is unimportant; consequently, the people can be found kowtowing to the images of both Buddhist and Taoist deities. A complete list of these deities would number into the tens of thousands.

There is a god for every occupation, even for beggars and thieves; a god of fire; gods of rain and thunder; a god of the kitchen and a god of wealth; a god of war and god of medicine; gods of sun, moon and stars; and the most popular deity is Guan-yin, the Goddess of Mercy.

We came upon myriad images of these deities, all attesting to the superstition and idolatry of the people. As we passed from one hideous figure to another, we were reminded of the Psalmist's comment on the vanity of idols:

> The idols of the nations are but silver and gold, the work of man's hands. They have mouths, but they do not speak; they have eyes, but they do not see; they have ears, but they do not hear; nor is there any breath at all in their mouth. Those who make them will be like them, yes, everyone who trusts in them (Psa. 135:15-18).

While Lucille turned away in horror, I stood in a cold sweat in the hall of one temple and watched the ordination of a number of young novitiates into the Buddhist priesthood. With heads shaven clean and a wild yell on their lips, they rushed into the hall and knelt at the feet of the priests in charge. Nine small lumps of incense were placed in rows of three on the head of each candidate and then ignited.

Uttering prayers and munching on tangerines in an effort to dull the pain, the novices continued to kneel while the burning incense ate its way into the flesh, leaving a nine-scar brand of the priesthood on their scalps. To wince or cry out in pain would have indicated a lack of zeal on the part of those being ordained. But not a sigh was heard as they strove to maintain the ardor of their priestly calling. Unfortunately for Buddhism, the loss of this ardor on the part of its priesthood is quite a common thing and thus the reason for the old saying, "Maintain the ardor of your priestly novitiate, and it will be more than enough to make you a Buddha." To reach that state of Buddhahood is the final goal of every earnest young novitiate.

As I watched this Buddhist rite, I was reminded of my own ordination and the fervor which was mine on that occasion. I was quick to realize that only with such fervor could I be used of God to help these "blind leaders of the blind" and turn them from "darkness to light and from the power of Satan unto God" (Acts 26:18).

Not only are the Chinese proud of their idols but they also pride themselves in their use of magic charms for every need—charms on the doors of homes to protect against demons; charms for the poor as well as the rich; charms for the sick; charms for the traveler on his way; charms for the living and charms for the dead; charms for this and that and everything else.

We also noticed that surrounding the temples were little shops featuring miniature paper rickshas, airplanes, servants, money, and numerous other objects which the Chinese religiously buy and burn in the belief that whatever they burn will become the real thing for their ancestors to use in the next world.

The superstition and idolatry was especially pronounced in the older generation; yet, as we passed through one temple after another, we began to note how the younger generation seemed to be forsaking not only the beliefs but also the customs and traditions of the older one. A look at the vast number of young people showing little reverence for these "houses of the gods" made us wonder why the priests didn't rise up with whips and drive them out, not that we had any liking for these "temples of Satan."

Why the shelving of religion in China? Why the profaning of temples? Why the dust on the altars of Buddhism? The answer can be found in the doubt and skepticism which accompanied China's great intellectual revolution which started in 1911 with the overthrow of the Manchu Dynasty. It seems now that the great spiritual conflict in China is not so much between Christianity and idolatry as between Christianity and a poisonous atheism which is slowly but surely causing the people to lose their sense of and craving for religion. Without a doubt, the present struggle is a much harder one than the former. This struggle is taking place in China today, and it was taking place when we first entered China many years ago. I felt at the time that the extent to which I could share in the struggle was in direct proportion to my measure of dedication, knowledge of the customs, and understanding of the language. This is why I was eager to start my studies in the Missionary Training School in Sichuan's fertile Chengdu Plain. And this is why it was so important that "I tarry in the plain."

"IT IS A LAND OF IDOLS"

Chapter 8

"I TARRY IN THE PLAIN"

"See, I will tarry in the plain of the wilderness, until there come word from you to inform me."
(2 Sam. 15:28 NKJV)

As David of old was forced to await certification by tarrying in the plain, even so was I forced to tarry in the Chengdu Plain until senior missionaries and language teachers certified that I was ready for work on the western border in Xikang Province. But getting to that plain was a problem in itself. For weeks we had waited as one thing after another hindered our transportation to the city of Chengdu in Sichuan Province.

The Bensons and Ralph Covell had managed to find accomodations on a rat-infested freighter and started up the Yangtze River on February 1, 1946. The rest of us were not so fortunate. The Chinese Government stepped in and commandeered all available river steamers to transport troops nearer Communist territory.

Since surface transportation was out, we investigated the possibility of flying to Chengdu on the *St. Paul*, the Lutheran World Federation's C-47. Happily enough, space was available and bookings were made. But right in the midst of our flight preparations word came through that the plane had developed mechanical trouble and was in need of an overhaul which would take a month or two.

As a last resort, we secured reservations on a China National Airline Corporation's plane for February 7th. Even that fell through when the government placed a temporary ban on all air passenger service while it investigated the reason for over a hundred lives being lost in plane crashes within a period of thirty days.

The ban went into effect immediately after the crash of a C.N.A.C plane near Hankow on January 28th, killing twenty-five persons. Eleven of the people killed on that plane were missionaries and their children. Several of them were supposed to have flown to Chengdu with us on the Lutheran Mission plane. But they tired of waiting and decided to go by a commercial plane. Among them were Mr. & Mrs. Robert Vick who with their two small children had come to China for the first time and were on their way to Chengdu for a period of language study. Little Paul Vick was the sole survivor of the crash and was rushed to the Country Hospital in Shanghai while I was still a patient there.

Hospital officials told me there was a fire aboard the plane. Since no parachutes were available, Bob Vick jumped from the plane, hoping to save his child by cushioning the impact with his own body. Those who rushed to the scene found the child in fairly good condition. Bob had saved his son's life and somehow managed to stay alive just long enough to identify himself, tell what had happened, and give final instructions concerning his child. Fortunately, there were those among the rescuers who could understand English.

The news of the Vick's Home-going came as a shock to those of us who had enjoyed their company aboard the *Marine Lynx* and were looking forward to further fellowship with them at the Missionary Training School in Chengdu. We were reminded again of our farewell visit with them at the Blackstone Apartments on the evening before their flight. We had been scratched from the passenger list of this same flight the day before it took off. Since fatal plane crashes had been so numerous, we thought it not strange for the Vicks to mention the possibility of their not reaching Chengdu. But the thing that did impress us was their willingness to leave that possibility with the Lord. Their boldness in wanting Christ to be magnified in their bodies either by life or by death stirred our hearts and caused us to question our own measure of dedication.

Things were really running at a low ebb when the business manager of the China Inland Mission was finally able to arrange for us to fly to Chengdu on two U.S. Army C-54s with bucket seats and a parachute for each passenger. He secured two flights for us on the 10th and 11th of March; and since I was the mission treasurer, he had me write out a check and instructed me to take it to the officer in charge. The contract was signed and our long period of waiting in Shanghai was over. We learned much later that the officer in question was to be disciplined for pocketing the money that the mission societies had paid him to fly their missionaries around China. We were also told that the U.S. Army was not in the business of furnishing civilian transportation. Be that as it may, legal or illegal, we were finally able to fly on to West China.

The plan was for me to go on ahead and make arrangements for the arrival of the main party. I went out on the first flight with a team of American soldiers. Lifting its wings above cosmopolitan Shanghai, our plane flew swiftly over lesser cities, made miles and miles of rice paddies look like cobblestone walks and dwarfed the rugged hills that jutted roughly into the air. Hours later our plane circled the city of Chengdu which was about 1200 miles to the west (as the crow flies) and landed in an open field which soon became filled with friendly-looking people to whom the foreigner and his ways were still an oddity.

My arrival on the outskirts of Chengdu with that military team was a memorable one. None of us on the plane could speak Chinese and no one knew how to request local transportation from U.S. Army Headqaurters in the city. The problem was finally solved when I found the remains of a telephone in a little mud hut at the end of the airstrip. Using sign language I got my point across to two rough-looking characters who apparently had charge of the telephone.

While one fellow fooled around with a pile of wires and batteries, the other squared off at an old-fashioned meat grinder of a telephone on a partial wall, twisted its tail a few times and began to yell, "Wei,wei,wei" right into the mouthpiece. He finally made contact with Headquarters and winked at his American audience to show hope and waited. After five or ten minutes, he shrugged his shoulders and hung up. That was strike one.

The next time it was a ball since the line fizzled out completely. They tinkered with the power plant, got it to work, and then tried again. This time they actually got a connection, but it broke before they could complete their message.

After a few more strikes and balls, they finally reached U.S. Army Headquarters and handed the phone to me. A veritable hailstorm was taking place in the receiver when I took hold of it, but I did hear an English-speaking voice on the other end of the line and yelled for transportation to town. Hours later that transportation did arrive. Such was the beginning of many series of strikes and balls which characterized missionary life and work in West China.

U.S. Army Headquarters had notified Ralph Covell and the Bensons of my arrival, and they rented vehicles and came to the airport to pick me up along with the baggage belonging to all of our missionaries. The following day we all went to the airport to pick up the rest of our missionary party. How good it was to be together again. The only person missing was Lee Lovegren who stayed in Shanghai to wait for the arrival of the Jim Garrisons.

As we "jeeped" our way through Chengdu we saw narrow streets lined with open shops and filled with people whose dress and manners might easily have marked them as "country cousins" of their Shanghai countrymen. Scores of ricksha boys hugged the sides of the roads and laughed at the still unfamiliar sight of "horseless and humanless carriages" passing through their streets, and countless children lined the walks to greet us with upheld thumbs and friendly "ding-hao's" (very good). Thanks to the American "G.I.," the bitter shout of "foreign devil" in West China was slowly but surely giving way to the more friendly "very good."

A very cordial welcome at the China Inland Mission compound in Chengdu proved to be the "pot of gold" awaiting us at the end of our journey's "rainbow." How remarkable it seemed to us that in so short a time we could be transported so many miles to a place so different and remote. Our stay of several weeks at the C.I.M. was filled with blessings as the folk there went out of their way to arrange their daily schedule to meet our language school schedule.

Our schedule in Chengdu called for us to mount our bicycles each morning, and, with our bells continually ringing out a warning, make our way through the rough, narrow streets, wondering if we'd reach our destination without knocking over a beggar, Buddhist priest, or some other pedestrian.

Traffic cops were to be found at almost every intersection, even ones with very little in the way of traffic, and they ruled the corner with an iron hand. A push-cart would come lumbering down the street at one mile per hour, the man pushing it clapping two pieces of bamboo together and holding up his hand to indicate that he wanted to make a right-hand turn. The cop would spin around to face him, look left, then right, shoot out one hand to hold up the non-existent traffic on the cross street, toot his whistle, and then with his other hand he'd wave the push-cart through. Then, and only them, would the cart make the turn. It was the same with all other forms of transportation—water buffalo carts, rickshas, pedicabs, bicycles and an occasional military jeep or truck.

The Lord saw fit in His good pleasure to answer our prayer for living quarters closer to the language school. In fact, He provided a large two-story missionary residence with a broad veranda right on the school campus. It was big enough to accomodate our group of five couples and one single man. The first few weeks in our new home were busy ones with luggage and freight to be unpacked, furniture to be bought, stove to be put up, windows and doors to be screened, rooms to be put in order, and a million and one other things to be done in order to make a house a home.

In the midst of all this was our language study and "time-wasting" afternoon tea parties. Why did the British have to introduce this Chinese custom to the foreign community in China? Every time we turned around, an ivitation to tea seemed to be staring us in the face. It seemed as though tea-drinking was the main occupation on that Christian campus. Tea! Tea! Tea! And I couldn't stand the stuff. Now, if it had been Coca Cola, I might have reconsidered the situation.

As far as the Chinese were concerned, I had nothing against their tea-drinking habit. To them, tea is "the cup that cheers but does not inebriate." And I will have to admit that the well-known character of the Chinese for temperance has been ascribed to their universal use of tea. It would be good if people in western lands would follow the custom of the Chinese in this respect instead of soaking themselves with beer. But there were many other Chinese customs that I didn't like and I was often quite vocal in criticizing them. In fact, Lee Lovegren thought I was a little bit too vocal, so he took me aside one day and kindly said, "Dan, it might be wise for you to learn a little more about Chinese customs before you condemn them. How well you learn them and observe them may determine the success or failure of your ministry here in China. One of the reasons for your study here at the Missionary Training School is to help you 'to be expert in all customs.'"

"I TARRY IN THE PLAIN"

"ME? A MISSIONARY?"

Chapter 9

"TO BE EXPERT IN ALL CUSTOMS"

> *"I think myself happy, King Agrippa, because I shall answer for myself this day before thee concerning all the things of which I am accused of the Jews, especially because I know thee to be expert in all customs and questions which are among the Jews." (Acts 26:2,3 NKJV)*

    I should have taken my cue from that old expert in customs, King Agrippa, but I didn't. Whereas he sought to influence his people by becoming an expert in their customs, I sought to influence mine by trying to substitute my customs for theirs. Somehow I was of the rather conceited opinion that the sooner the Chinese adopted western ways the better it would be for them and the whole world in general. The folly of such an opinion led me down a bitter road of embarrassment.

    One of my first mishaps on that road grew out of an innocent little shopping tour. I was busily minding my own business of being a pack animal for my wife when a beggar rushed up and started panhandling her in a very rough fashion. With good old American gallantry, I dashed to the rescue and lifted the fellow away from her. Imagine my surprise when the old rascal deliberately fell on the ground and cried out for the sympathy of passers-by. Why, you'd think I had beaten him within an inch of his life. At least his wild antics suggested as much.

    In record time, we had our jury of a hundred or more people and the trial began. My inability to speak the language forced me into the role of the defendant and what a sorry mess I made out of it. My gesticulatory defense brought nothing but looks of contempt from those who were hearing the case. Their eyes seemed to be saying, "Why you high-nosed foreign devil, what's the big idea of striking a poor, defenseless beggar?" If those same eyes had only known that I was a foreign missionary, I'm sure they would have said, "If that's your way of spreading the Gospel of Love, then we want no part of it!"

It was too late to use the time-honored Chinese custom of enlisting a passer-by to act as a middleman. It was also too late to fall back on the customary practice of "talking it out." In my case, it would have been "acting it out" since I couldn't handle the language. Such customs had always seemed ridiculous to me, especially the latter one.

I had seen a number of Chinese street fights which consisted of two enraged people standing face to face and presumably calling each other every foul name in the Chinese vocabulary, the object being to get the other fellow to throw the first punch. This I had figured out for myself. What I didn't know was that the fellow who threw the first punch would invariably be considered the guilty party while the recipient of the blow would reap the reward of the innocent and gain the favor of the crowd. As for me and my case, I was supposed to have struck the man. Actually, I had merely grabbed him and lifted him away from my wife, but there was no convincing the crowd of this fact.

I was right in the midst of wishing that I were ten thousand miles away from that spot when a policeman who was well-acquainted with the false antics of my "accuser" walked up and chased him away, apparently regretting the fact that we had been disturbed. With a big sigh of relief, I welcomed, like any good Chinese person, the restoration of "face" and resolved from that moment on to keep my hands off the Chinese. I should have learned this long before when I visited China as a Navy chaplain. I often noticed how terribly offended the Chinese were when American sailors would swagger down the street, put their arms around the Chinese, and say, "How are you, buddy?" These servicemen considered the Chinese very lucky to have them on their side and they wanted the Chinese to know it. I couldn't blame the Chinese for thinking that Americans were very uncouth and inconsiderate of their customs. These American servicemen should have followed the example of the British servicemen who, for the most part, respected the Chinese and their ways and kept their hands off of them.

I must confess that I was certainly learning Chinese customs the hard way. Undoubtedly the way would have been much easier had I been willing to listen to the advice of my senior missionaries. I should have shown more interest in the old Chinese adage, "Faithful advice is harsh to the ear, but is of advantage to the conduct; good medicine is bitter to the taste, but it cures the disease." But how to distinguish between good advice and bad advice from a city full of old China missionaries who disagreed among themselves as to custom posed a real problem. Actually, there was an element of truth in all that they had to say, but many of them were unwilling to admit that the familiar customs of the locale in which they labored stood a good chance of not being accepted in other areas.

It's true that a number of customs are acceptable throughout all the land of China, yet there are some customs that are peculiar only to a particular area and some are peculiar only to a certain level of society within that area. It's not unusual, therefore, to find the coastal Chinese laughing at the customs of the inland Chinese and vice versa. And the more modernized Chinese in larger cities can often be found ridiculing the ancient customs of their country cousins just a few miles away.

The question that faced me was just how was I to determine local custom from general custom. One thing was sure, I didn't want anyone to catch me observing some outdated custom in a modern locale. I certainly would have looked stupid walking along the streets of Shanghai with my wife humbly trailing along several paces behind me or knocking my head on the sidewalk in a kowtow to someone of superior rank—the louder the impact, the greater the respect. As it was, a bit of bad advice from one senior missionary led me to put a ban on my wife's practice of taking my arm as we walked down the streets of Shanghai together, but one look at the number of Chinese couples walking along arm-in-arm prompted me to lift the ban.

On the other hand, I didn't want to be caught being too modern in an area observing ancient customs. It's true that certain polite forms were changed after the Revolution of 1911; yet not so much, perhaps, as one might suppose. In fact, the late Dr. Omar L. Kilborn who taught for many years at our Missionary Training School in Chengdu once said:

A practical knowledge of the common forms of politeness that prevail among the Chinese is essential to good relations between them and the missionary and to the best influence of the missionary in his great task of giving them the Gospel.

"ME? A MISSIONARY?"

"Chinese Politeness is based on real respect... love and desire to be agreeable."

Chinese politeness, like that of other countries, is based on real respect and love, on the desire to be agreeable, and to be tactful and helpful. No missionary can afford to despise it, or even to regard it lightly. While we may not hope to perfect ourselves in all the many ramifications of Chinese etiquette, in all the many details, we can by care and attention in observation and practice, acquire such a familiarity with the main principles that we shall be able to make ourselves and our Chinese friends feel at ease on ordinary occasions; that we shall not often outrage the Chinese sense of that which is fitting; that we shall, in other words, make the very most of

"TO BE EXPERT IN ALL CUSTOMS"   71

polite forms as a powerful, extraneous aid to the setting up of the Kingdom.

This careful reasoning on the part of Dr. Kilborn caused me to pay more attention to this matter of Chinese politeness. I found an opportune time to practice it when a Chinese cyclist accidentally bumped into me and both of us hit the hard pavement. The little fellow was petrified with fear and fully expected me to read him off, but imagine his surprise when I helped him to his feet and bothered myself about his well-being. The incident resulted in his inviting me to a cup of tea and a crowd cheering me for giving him a hand. I was quite puffed up over my newly acquired ability to get along with the Chinese until that day when we young missionaries accompanied our senior missionary, Lee Lovegren, to a banquet held in our honor at one of the civic halls in the city of Chengdu. Important bank officials had invited us to the banquet in order to welcome us to the city. Of course we were fully aware of the fact that this generosity on the part of these officials also had its customary place. This was their way of showing us that they would appreciate our patronage of their bank in the future.

As we walked into the banquet hall, Lee advised us to split up and sit at different tables. It wouldn't look good for us foreigners to be sitting together at a table by ourselves. I noticed an empty place at a table on the far side of the room. I also noticed two distinguished-looking Chinese gentlemen pushing each other around at the head of the table, but I didn't pay too much attention to them since I was more interested in eating. Since I was quite hungry, I went over and sat down in that empty seat and began to help myself to the food. Just as soon as I sat down, those two men stopped their fighting.

As we were leaving the banquet hall that night, Lee came up to me and said, "Dan, you broke a very important Chinese custom tonight." My reply was, "How? By simply sitting down and eating with those people?" His answer was, "Yes! Did you notice those two distinguished-looking gentlemen pushing each other around at the head of your table? Well, they were trying to carry out an old Chinese custom of important people trying to push each other into the seat of honor which is the seat farthest away from the main entrance to the hall. While they were in the process of observing this custom, you came along and sat right down in the seat of honor, so these top officials had nothing left to fight about."

You can imagine how embarrassed I was to hear my senior missionary complaining about my actions that night and telling me that my behavior was a wonderful way of losing friends and alienating people. I say it to my shame that I complained about his way of setting me straight. Yes, I found myself saying with David of old, "I am restless in my complaint."

"TO BE EXPERT IN ALL CUSTOMS"

"All in favor of Chinese food once a day raise your hand."

Chapter 10

"I AM RESTLESS IN MY COMPLAINT"

"Give ear to my prayer, O God; and do not hide Thyself from my supplication. Give heed to me, and answer me; I am restless in my complaint and am surely distracted." (Psa. 55:1,2)

David had an awful lot to complain about to God, but his complaints were far more legitimate than my complaints on the Chengdu Plain. There were a number of things that I didn't like about the way my fellow missionaries did things, and they certainly didn't like a lot of things that I did.

An old Chinese proverb claims that "each man has his own mind, and each mind has its own viewpoint." Truer words were never spoken. No sooner had we settled down in our new home when all of us began expressing our own points of view. And when Jim and Virginia Garrison joined our missionary family a few months later, there were exactly eleven viewpoints to be considered. Fortunately, the two children in the house, Linn Ann Simpson and Dan Carr, Jr., were too young to express theirs. Considering that we had come from all over the United States and from entirely different backgrounds, it's a wonder that we got along as well as we did—staid Easterners, blunt Mid-Westerners, wild Westerners, each claiming that his or her point of view was the best.

And to think that I had the audacity to suggest that the George Cole and Elwyn Stafford families plus Flora Mae Duncan move in with us upon their arrival in the near future. What a happy situation that would have been—fifteen adults and five children all under the same roof.

The hopeless task of trying to please us all fell on the shoulders of our senior missionaries, Lee and Ida Lovegren. Never in all their years in China had it been their lot to ride herd on such a wild bunch of raw recruits. Some wanted to do this and some wanted to do that. Some wanted a watch dog while others wanted a cat. Some wanted to fire the gateman. Others wanted to keep him and raise his salary. Some felt that we should restrict compound visitors while others felt the main gate should be left wide open and were quick to advise that we should be available to visitors twenty-four hours per day. If not, the people would stay away from us, thinking that we didn't want to be bothered with them. Unfortunately, this was true in many cases.

"Never in all their years in China had Lee and Ida Lovegren such a herd of raw recruits"

The story continues with some missionaries wanting a garden and others thinking it was too much of a good thing. Some wanted this kind of food and others wanted that kind. Some wanted meat at every meal while others wanted it just once a day. Some thought we should have Chinese food at least once a day. Others were in favor of having Chinese food once a week and American food the rest of the time.

Some wanted to retire early at night while others wanted to burn the midnight oil. Some wanted our daily devotional service in the morning. Others wanted it at night. Some favored burning coal while others favored wood or charcoal. This differing of opinions finally resulted in a happy solution. Each family would take turns at running the household for a month even though it meant a change in diet at the changing of each shift.

"I AM RESTLESS IN MY COMPLAINT"   77

The Garrisons encountered a real problem during one of their shifts. Some began to complain that there was too much water in the milk and wanted Jim to talk to the milkman. This was a common complaint in our town since many milkmen were guilty of watering down their product. The situation was so bad that customers began buying lactometers and testing their milk each day. Well, Jim did talk to the milkman and the man denied that he had been watering down the milk. In fact, we almost fell over in laughter when the milkman arrived the next day with his mooing cow and demanded that we test the milk right there on the spot. This incident helped to relieve some of the tension between us. The milk passed the test.

"It is easy to get acquainted, but it is difficult to live together for a long time." We should have been aware of this Chinese proverb, but we weren't. Some of us felt that our difficulty in living together was due to the many weary miles we had left behind us. Sickness along the road hadn't helped any either. Blame was also attached to the amount of energy we expended in trying to adapt to the unfamiliarity of it all, particularly in trying to catch on to the Chinese way of doing things. For example, their custom of haggling over prices led consciously or unconsciously to a level of anxiety after each encounter. Every single purchase transaction was raised to the level of negotiating the Treaty of Versailles. Nearly every tradesman or merchant states the price of his goods with a view to getting as much as he possibly can. As a general rule, it is quite safe to presume that he is asking a quarter or a third more than he expects to receive. The strategy is to offer him half of what he asks; then, while he gradually reduces his price, gradually raise your offer until neutral ground is reached. Finally, split the difference and he will probably be glad to take what you give him.

This must all be done with a perfect nonchalance. No eagerness to obtain the object must be shown. No word of praise for the product must fall from your lips. Any little defect in it must be pointed out. As the old proverb says, "'Bad, bad,' says the buyer; but when he goes his way, then he boasts."

When in doubt as to the value of anything, a very good plan is to haggle over the price of the same article in several other shops. A pretty shrewd guess may then be made as to what is a fair value for the article. When a salesman sees a customer on the point of leaving his shop, he will come down to nearly, if not quite, as low a figure as he is prepared to accept. In his thinking, anyone who pays the first price asked deserves to be fleeced.

The Chinese love a bargain and find a positive pleasure in haggling over the price, which the foreigner can scarcely appreciate. Viewed from a westerner's tendency toward social insularity, it represents an uncomfortable and unnecessary point of social confrontation. The fact that we were barely able to communicate only exacerbated the frustration. It wasn't until much later that I became a real expert in the art of haggling. The day would come when even my Chinese friends would ask me to haggle for them.

On the other hand, my little wife shunned the habit of haggling as much as possible. Had it not been for my complaints, she would have given any and all merchants the first price asked and let it go at that. Needless to say, she much preferred shopping alone and dreaded the thought of tagging along with me. However, being a courageous soul, she did accompany me at times and blushed at the way I operated. I was determined to be an expert in this custom.

"I AM RESTLESS IN MY COMPLAINT"

The unloading of our freight also added to our woes. Pilferage had claimed some of it, and that which did arrive was badly damaged. Yet, after 2,000 miles by steamer, truck, and coolie power, it was a miracle that it arrived at all. I can still hear that coolie cry as he pushed our 400-pound stove off the back of the truck, "Well, that's the last of it." And I can still hear the rattle of broken parts and see chips of enamel pouring through the cracks of our stove crate.

Even though we tried to live peaceably with one another, we found it an ever-present necessity to confess our faults one to another. Be it to our credit, we were sometimes able to fulfill the message of that old oriental dictum which exhorts us to "endure provocation, repress anger, forgive an offense, and yield a point." In fact, a number of missionaries from other societies marveled at the way we got along in our "happy" home.

With all of the confusion and weariness of travel and trying to adapt to our new home, I was sometimes prone to take care of secular matters first. I placed much of the blame on the fact that I just had too much to do. Somehow I felt like extra weight, not accomplishing anything. Furthermore, opportunities for witnessing among the Chinese were limited. Many souls around me were lost and dying, and I could do very little to help them find the Way of Life because I couldn't speak their language. In this very strange land "I heard a language that I did not know."

Chapter 11

"I HEARD A LANGUAGE THAT I DID NOT KNOW"

"He established it for a testimony in Joseph, when he went throughout the land of Egypt. I heard a language that I did not know." (Psa. 81:5)

Speaking for the Children of Israel who had been taken captive in Egypt, the Psalmist looks back in time and says, "I heard a language that I did not know." This foreign language was one of the many frustrations of their condition in Egypt.

Not being able to understand the language was also one of my big frustrations as I started my work in China. After my first day of language study, I turned to my wife and said, "The Chinese language sounds to me like a combination of snake-hisses and throat gargling set to music and sung with a mouth full of mush, but just give me time and I'll get it."

My wife's reaction to our first day in language school was quite different than mine. With tears in her eyes, she cried, "Dan, I'll never be able to speak the language. Why I can't even make the sounds let alone recognize the tones and grasp the grammar." But despite her initial pessimism, she was soon taking to the language like a duck to water while I who had been so optimistic at the start had to get it the hard way—with blood, sweat, and jeers. I had staked my hopes of getting the language on Psalm 81:10, "Open your mouth wide and I will fill it." Unfortunately, I opened my mouth wide, but no Chinese came out of it.

Since the laughs, as far as the language was concerned, were usually on me, I got it back on the "Little Lady" one day when she went up on a tone instead of down and discovered later that the cook had prepared refreshments for forty guests on Thursday instead of Sunday.

Yes, we made numerous mistakes, but God was good in quickening our minds to the task and indeed showed great patience with "Yours Truly." I still question the old Chinese axiom which says, "Devote much attention to the language. Every character is worth a thousand pieces of gold."

Unfortunately, I had accepted the job of field treasurer while studying the language and wasn't able to devote all of my attention to it. This set me back for quite some time. I finally resigned the job in frustration in order to devote more time to the study of the language.

William Carey, the first Protestant missionary to India, encouraged new missionaries to put everything else aside and give full attention to language study. How sorry I feel for those missionaries who are constantly diverted from their language study by "extra-curricular" activities—even by teaching English Bible classes.

They delude themselves, as I did, with the thought that there was plenty of time to get the language. Soon, however, they become burdened down with so many activities and preaching through interpreters that they never really become fluent in the language. Many end up as failures and head back to their home countries.

There was a time when I thought I could overcome the language problem in a hurry. While walking down a street in Chengdu, I saw a little Chinese book store and, naturally, I went in and looked around. Show me the minister who doesn't enter a bookstore when he sees one.

Most of the books were in Chinese, but suddenly I saw a little book in English entitled *A Shortcut to the Chinese Language*. It was a pamphlet that had been published during World War II for American servicemen stationed in the Orient—a U.S. Army publication. It was an English-Chinese phrase book. The Chinese phrases were spelled out phonetically.

I bought that little book and went on my way saying to myself, "What a surprise my language teachers are going to get. Why, I'll probably be preaching my first sermon in a few months." Little did I realize the problems I would have with that book.

With volume in hand, I sallied forth. Everything went well until I came to a military sentry box. A man in uniform leaned out and mumbled something as I sauntered by with a "ding hao (very good)" toss of the wrist. A moment later he let out a yell and I heard the unmistakable click of a rifle bolt. Spinning around, I saw him leveling his rifle at me and I demanded, in English of course, the reason for his rude behavior.

"I HEARD A LANGUAGE THAT I DID NOT KNOW"   83

Pointing his gun at me, he read me off in terms that called for my little *Shortcut to the Chinese Language*. I pulled it out and found an appropriate phrase, "What do you want?" Looking across at the Chinese characters with the phonetics underneath, I began reading the phrase, hoping the sentry would understand me. No matter how many times I read that phrase, using the Chinese tones in different combinations, he still had a blank look on his face.

Finally, I put my finger on the Chinese characters and held the book right up before his nose. Fortunately, he was one of the few people who could read his own language. With a new look of understanding on his face, he took the book out of my hands. After finding an appropriate military expression, he placed his finger on the Chinese characters and put the book right in front of my nose. Looking across at the English equivalent, I read, "Halt, or I'll fire!" I halted! Things were not as "ding hao" as I thought. Apparently, I had been walking right into a military restricted zone.

Overcoming an odd feeling in the pit of my stomach and leafing frantically through the book, I found "Pardon me." The sentry, in turn, found "O.K." and waved me on my way in the opposite direction. The result of all this was my "retiring" that little book and going back to language school to get the language the "hard" way. I finally came to the realization that there was no shortcut to the Chinese language.

I'm afraid I found little comfort in the words of our senior missionary, "Dan, Chinese is actually very simple. Unlike English, difficult grammatical forms are few." It wasn't the grammatical forms that bothered me. It was the tonal quality of the language. In one of our missionary letters, Lucille wrote, "Dan is having the time of his life helping out on the 'singing end of the line.' I'm convinced that his hilarity in this respect is due to the fact that a person doesn't have to worry about tones when singing Chinese."

Tones! Tones! I still remember the time a little ruffian hit me in the back of the neck with a large rock. I chased him down four streets, across a stream, through three alleys, up two flights of stairs, and right into the arms of his mother.

I raised my voice and told the mother that her son was mischievous. At least that's what I thought I told her; but, instead of getting angry, she smiled at me. And the more I spoke, the more she smiled. Why did she smile? Well, our Chinese evangelist gave me the answer to that question later that day. When I told him what I thought I had said, he replied, "You were not telling the mother that her son was mischievous, you were telling her that her son was not mischievous—same pronunciation, wrong tone." No wonder she smiled.

There was also the time I memorized a short five-minute sermon for delivery at a nearby church. The sermon included repeated pleas to believe in the Lord. This is what I thought I was saying; yet, each time I repeated the plea, the laughter increased—as well as my confusion. It wasn't until the end of the service that a deacon politely informed me that I had been using the word "pig" instead of the word "Lord." No ordinary Chinese person would ever confuse "ju," a first tone word meaning "pig" with "ju," a fourth tone word meaning "Lord," but I did (Western Mandarin tones).

Though most of our time in language school was necessarily spent in acquiring the spoken language, there were also times when we were forced to splash out Chinese characters with a Chinese writing brush. It was a long time before these scratchings of a cross-eyed bird began to make sense. At least I was right in thinking that they had something to do with nature, for I learned that a legendary figure by the name of Dzang-jieh who lived about 2700 B.C. is credited with the invention of symbols to represent ideas in writing by noticing the markings on a turtle shell, thus imitating objects in nature. These symbols contain thousands of word pictures, some of them recognizable by a casual glance. We were surprised to learn that written Chinese is a picture language, not an alphabetical one.

My language study went on like perpetual motion. Day after day I repeated sentences after a somewhat distracted and weary teacher. How he winced at my floundering Chinese. One of those sentences made the profound observation that donkeys are slower than horses. I also repeated a very fascinating account of boxes being carried in and out of a house. The only sentence that really interested me was one having to do with the number of hairs on my head. It touched me in a very personal sort of way since my hair was disappearing at such a rapid rate that I was afraid I would soon be able to actually count the remaining ones.

My teachers found these sessions equally as boring. One of them actually fell asleep on me three times within an hour. I'm convinced that the only reason he stuck around with a salary of ten cents per day was in the hope that I would have a truck shipped out from the States for him to use in the tobacco business. Rarely did a day pass without this fellow finding an opportunity to raise the subject of his "American truck." Though he was as poor as the proverbial church mouse, he assured me that he would be able to pay back every cent from the certain profit he would reap in the tobacco hauling business.

Such was language study. I was worrying about the number of hairs on my head and the speed of donkeys when all about me precious souls were perishing for want of a Savior. The harsh but practical reality of language school is a necessary crucible for the almost naive enthusiasm of each new missionary. Doubt, confusion, and uncertainty are a part of the experience. At that particular time I was very much in need of a rest and a chance to readjust my footing. That's why I looked forward to our first summer vacation in China. What a summer it was. It is best described in the words of the prophet Amos, "And behold, there was a basket of summer fruit."

Chapter 12

"AND BEHOLD, THERE WAS A BASKET OF SUMMER FRUIT"

"Thus the Lord God showed me, and behold, there was a basket of summer fruit." (Amos 8:1)

Some of our Chinese friends were quick to inform us that we would never have beheld our basket of summer fruit had we observed the Lin Hsia Festival. Devoid of any religious importance, the Lin Hsia Festival marks the beginning of Summer. On this day Chinese children are dressed in linen and made to sit on all of the thresholds in the home to ward off summer illnesses. They are also made to eat eggs in the belief that the "sons of chickens," as eggs are known in the north, will keep them from contracting summer diseases.

Our particular basket of summer fruit reminded us of that basket of summer judgments seen by the prophet Amos only ours consisted of one trying experience after another. The contents of that basket included sickness. First, Dan, Jr., became bedridden with a combination of whooping cough, measles, and ch'i poisoning (similar to poison ivy) and was followed soon after by Lucille when she contracted a bad case of typhus.

Hoping to forego the remaining contents of that basket, we sought the counsel of veteran missionaries. Their advice was for us to leave the inopheles mosquitoes and heat of the Chengdu Plain and head sixty miles northwest to Beiluding (White Deer Summit), a lone peak located behind the first range of mountains at the western rim of the plain. In ancient times it was a place of refuge.

Since Lucille and Irene Simpson, along with the children, had been offered a ride in what used to be an automobile, the rest of us, not being so fortunate, decided to leave a few days in advance by ricksha and bicycle. We figured on a two-day trip while those going by auto figured on four hours. It was our plan to arrive just early enough to prepare a cabin before the mothers and children arrived.

Though the morning of our planned departure for the summit was darkened by rain clouds, we started out. Traveling by bike was compulsory for the men in our party since no ricksha men were willing to pull our weight for sixty miles over rough, dirt roads and through a number of streams. We had to push our bikes most of the way over roads which didn't deserve to be called roads. And rain, mud and slush were our constant companions. Meals were found in little town restaurants with dirt floors and shared with the resident dogs, cats, chickens, rats, bugs, flies, fleas and lice. Brooms were unnecessary for cleaning up scraps.

What a relief it was to get out into the countryside left fresh and green by the many rains. We rejoiced to see the many full fields of rice which promised to relieve the rice shortage in Chengdu, a shortage which had caused numerous riots and some deaths.

One cannot ride far without coming to little villages—small clusters of stores and houses with their thatched roofs blending into nature's picture. Numerous compounds with their mud or bamboo walls made a pretty picture as they stood out like little islands in the rice paddies.

Even the people seemed to belong to the scenery. Their straw hats, grass sandals, and capes made from the bark of trees together with the inevitable blue and black of their clothing blended with the landscape. But as one looked more carefully and saw the crowding, the poverty, and the uncared for diseases in quarters small and filthy, he couldn't help but realize how completely out of harmony their lives were with the God of nature. The drawn, passive faces of the aged scarred by a lifetime of harsh struggle and suffering gave meaning to the phrase: "dead while they yet live." The countless wayside shrines that seemed to increase in number as we came nearer the mountains gave stark evidence to the fact that these people had no Comforter.

Our first day on the road ended with a race through the rain and darkness to the walled town of Peng-hsien. Robbers had been reported in the area. Though they actually climbed the walls and raided the town just the night before, we were still relieved to reach the confines of the town. The gates to the town were being closed for the night as we entered the place. It was quite an experience racing after sundown to reach the safety of the town walls. The ricksha men who were pulling the women in our party showed their fear by making probably the quickest time they had ever made in their lives.

While preparing to leave the morning of the second day, I reinjured the knee that had given me so much trouble in the Navy. This meant staying behind until other transportation for me could be found or pushing on, using my bike as a crutch. Naturally, I chose the latter and finally hobbled to the foot of the mountain, only to find that all of the bridges—logs tied together and anchored to trees on either side of the river—were washed out. This meant waiting in the little town of Haiozi for the waters to recede and also tasting again that basket of summer fruit. This time it was a case of dysentery which put me in bed with a high fever and all of the other discomforts that go with dysentery. It also meant frequent trips to the toilet which was located in a pig pen just outside the inn. It was nothing more than two slightly divided shaky planks of wood stretched across an open cesspool about six feet deep. On one of my frequent trips I almost met up with disaster when I slipped on one of the planks. Someone ahead of me had missed his target. A number of years later, my youngest son did slip into a similar cesspool and almost drowned.

After a four-day wait and still shaky on my legs, I climbed into a huagan—a piece of bamboo matting slung between two poles and usually carried by two men. In the case of my two hundred pounds, it was four men. They quickly informed me that I was too heavy for two men and there was a wide river to be crossed; so on we went on our final lap to White Deer Summit.

When we reached the river at the foot of the mountain, our carriers threw heavy stones into the water only to see them swept away by the fierce current. They finally concluded that the river was still too dangerous and prepared to head back to town. Lucille revealed the conclusion to this story in one of her missionary letters:

> When they reached the river, the mountain carriers thought it too treacherous to ford and started to turn back; but that husband of mine, not wishing to spend another two or three days waiting in Haiozi, climbed out of his huagan,

"AND BEHOLD, THERE WAS A BASKET ..." 91

fashioned a crutch from a tree limb, and started into the stream. The incident ended with him standing on the other side of that "uncrossable" river and challenging the carriers to follow. Having lost enough "face" already, their only alternative was to cross. All I can say is that Dan's guardian angel was more than generous to him that day. No wonder his latest song has been "Got any Rivers You Think are Uncrossable?"

Well, so much for Lucille's review of the situation. I must confess that I felt quite guilty for pushing the carriers on when one of them with a heavy load was swept down the river for about a quarter of a mile and finally saved himself by grabbing a large rock in the middle of the river. The poor fellow was bleeding profusely when other carriers finally rescued him.

After a good rest, I climbed back into my huagan and hung on for dear life as my carriers began a steady climb, slight at first but increasing until I wondered if it would be possible for the men to carry me almost straight up; but these were mountain men and well-qualified for the task.

Americans have often taken a great deal of delight in depicting the Chinese as slant-eyed people with long queues or pigtails running down their backs. Actually, such people are rarely seen in China today unless it be at White Deer Summit or some other out-of-the-way place. Why some Chinese have queues is far beyond the comprehension of Westerners.

It wasn't style or custom that caused Chinese to adopt this queue hair style during just the last three hundred years of their 4,000-year history. It was forced upon them by the foreign Manchus when they overthrew the Ming Dynasty in 1644. An order went out at that time for all Chinese men and women to shave their foreheads and wear a queue, the object being to "Manchu-nize" the Han or Chinese people. Failure to comply with the order meant death. Official barbers accompanied by executioners with broad-swords marched into the towns and forcibly shaved the foreheads of the people and made them wear queues. Those who objected were immediately beheaded. The practice was declared illegal and "theoretically" done away with when the Chinese Nationalists overthrew the Manchu Dynasty in 1911.

Although the ban on queues was not widely enforced, few people can be seen wearing them today. My huagan men were among the few and my feet caught in their hair as they carried me up the mountain. About half way up the mountain, we stopped at a Buddhist temple and sought food and lodging for the night. That night among the idols will linger long in my memory—priests moving about here and there and tending some thirty or forty idols, burning incense, chanting prayers, ringing bells and pounding gongs. What a strange experience! How my heart went out to them in their darkness. And there I was unable to tell them in their own tongue about the One who means the difference between light and darkness.

I was also surprised to see a number of children running about among the idols. Many of them were orphans and others had been given to the temple by their parents. There they studied for the priesthood.

The next day, the four men carrying me wore themselves out, leaving me to climb the last one thousand feet alone. All my protestations about still being weak from dysentery and having a bad knee didn't sway them one bit, so up I hobbled and finally collapsed

"AND BEHOLD, THERE WAS A BASKET..."

at the top. My mission was accomplished—nine days and sixty miles later.

Dr. Fritz Fisher who had arrived on the mountain top several days earlier splinted my leg and tucked me away in my room for the next six weeks. There I was flat on my back in the clouds wondering what had become of my wife and child. The last report concerning them revealed that they had been marooned in Chengdu. The river which ran behind our house jumped its banks and left our women and children surrounded by water which had already reached the depth of five feet. Suffice it to say, I was mighty relieved when Lucille walked into my room some two weeks later and told me the story. Here it is in her own words:

> Since Mrs. Simpson and I had been offered a ride in an automobile, Dan and the others went on to prepare the cabins, expecting us to follow in a few days. The few days, however, passed into two weeks, for the rain which dampened their departure continued. In fact, it still seems like a nightmare when I think of the rain pouring down unceasingly and the river rising until its banks could no longer contain it. The roaring of the river (a stone's throw from the rear of our house) and the steady beat of the rain faded into the background during the day and night as the screams and cries of frightened people filled the air. We heard them first when a nearby bridge collapsed, and it plus the people on it toppled into the rushing waters.
>
> As we looked from our balcony, we saw the bridge, houses and people, many household articles, and odd pieces of lumber being borne along in the swift current. People stood along the banks trying to salvage what they could of the debris. But as the day went into evening, even the most daring were driven back as the river rose higher and higher.
>
> We watched as the force of the water crumbled the walls which were six feet high and two feet thick and rushed madly into our compound. Our servants gathered belongings from their little houses and moved into our much higher and safer one. They huddled together in fear, expecting to see their homes washed away at any moment. The flood waters swept

into the missionary residence across the street from ours and caused its occupants to rush to the upper story.

We finally went to bed for the night, but the continual roaring coupled with crashes as something else bowed to the power of the maddened river made much sleep impossible. You can imagine how we felt with four or five feet of water on all sides of us and rising every minute. If ever I needed that verse, "What time I am afraid I will trust in Thee," I needed it then. Although the rain continued all through the night, the water reached its crest about 2:00 A.M. A few days later we learned that we had experienced perhaps the worst flood in the history of Chengdu. For the first time in its history, two locks had been opened at the Guanhsien Dam instead of one. Because of this, a number of people in the know had predicted a flood. Several hundred people lost their lives and countless numbers were left homeless.

"AND BEHOLD, THERE WAS A BASKET ..." 95

Finally the weather seemed favorable for us to start for White Deer Summit, but our chartered automobile could not make the trip since bridges had been washed out along the way. By this time, John Simpson and Lee Lovegren had returned from their survey trip into Xikang Province, our chosen field of work, so our party was increased to the five of us plus two amahs and our cook.

A Chinese friend suggested that we make the trip by horse cart. That sounded novel, so we asked for two of them to be at our house at 6:40 A.M. on July 14th. I anticipated a horse drawn wagon similar to one in the States; but when they arrived, late of course, I found them to be very small carts pulled by undersized horses that looked ready for the "boneyard." We soon found that the horses were capable of trotting no more than three minutes at a time and that at rare intervals. Their average pace? Well, we could have walked it more quickly. Nevertheless, we enjoyed it.

Foreigners are always an attraction and seemingly the horse cart increased the people's interest; for as we approached a village, one voice after another would shout, "Ma la che lai!" ("A horse cart is coming!") Grown-ups as well as children would dash out to see. After spotting our children, their cries would increase. We left one of the larger towns with about thirty children running alongside us for at least a mile. Little Dan had the time of his life laughing and "talking" to them. We stopped to eat at a Chinese restaurant along the way and were immediately surrounded. Since I'm still not too adept at using chopsticks, the audience was a little disconcerting; consequently, I consumed very little but Danny ate better than usual and enjoyed the crowd plus the many dogs at our feet.

After two days on the road, we reached Haiozi—a little town at the foot of the mountains—and found carriers waiting to take us to White Deer Summit the following day. The next morning, we boarded our huagans and started up the mountain. I really didn't like the idea, for I'm not yet accustomed to men taking the part of a beast of burden; but on we went, fording a river filled with rapids.

After the huagan men had rested, we started up narrow, winding paths from which we could see the valleys below and the mountains on every side rising as high as 15,000 feet, a panorama of majestic beauty. At last we reached our cottage on top of the mountain and found my long-lost husband. We also found a climate cool and invigorating and the promise of good fellowship with approximately thirty other missionaries. Although we made the trip in three days, Dan and the others were on the way nine days.

We were finally on the mountain top, but don't start concluding that we were there for just a rest. Far from it. We were there to get away from the heat and mosquitoes. Language study, perish the thought, went on as usual—more sentences about donkeys being slower than horses and more boxes being carried in and out while more unsaved people were being carried out to the cemetery each day. One of our veteran missionaries to India, Eric Frykenburg, was right when he said, "Here we are playing with paper dolls while the whole world is tumbling down around us."

As a general rule, the Chinese aren't bothered by noise. Complete quietness to them suggests gloom. To break the tranquility, they keep chirping insects. Many like to be "sung" to sleep with the insects going full blast. Would that I could say as much for myself. I had the time of my life trying to stay awake at language study during the daytime; but when I tried to get some real sleep at night, I was serenaded by a cacophony of insects of every kind and description—mosquitoes, gnats, moths, stingers, whizzers, hissers, hummers, whistlers, and the worst of all, cicadas with their infernal clickety clacking.

Confinement to bed on that mountain top, language study, insects, and then servants all combined to make my basket of summer fruit a very distasteful one. To say that our servants ran us a merry race is to put it mildly. From the very moment of their arrival they were ready to head back to Chengdu, but since they were compelled to stay, there was no end to their complaints and filching. Of course, they truly believed a little filching was part of their job. Money would be given them to purchase the daily groceries. After their return from the market place, they would give an accounting of their purchases, often inflating the figures and pocketing the balance.

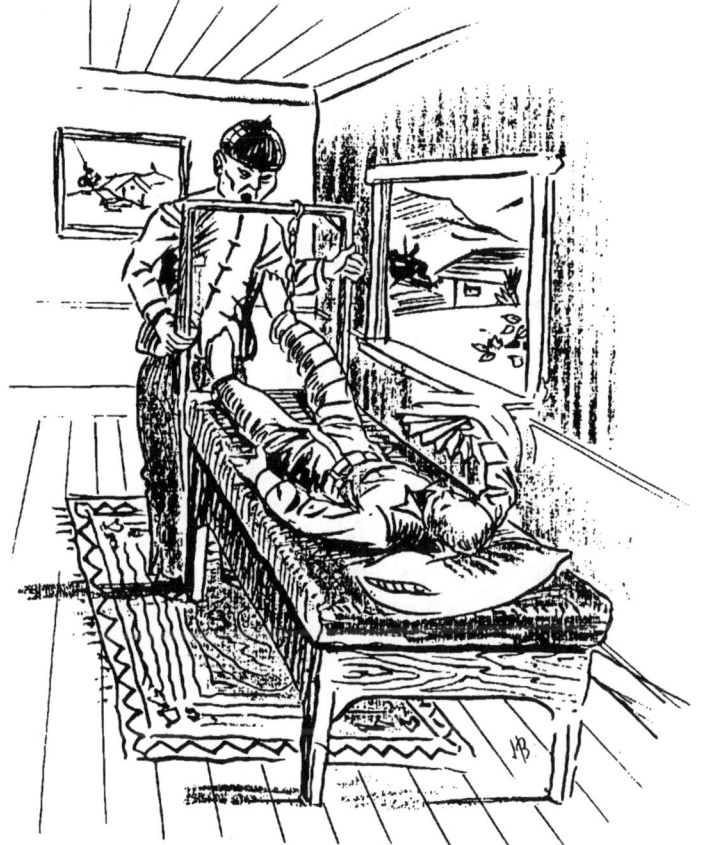

Despite the inflation, their grocery bill would usually be much less than the bill foreigners would pay if they themselves had gone out and made the same purchases. Of course, a foreigner would question the ethics of such a practice. In fact, one lady who was vacationing on the mountain became so irritated at the brazen filching by her cook that she slapped the fellow. This was a grave mistake. Women in that part of China just don't go around slapping men. A man feels more offended when slapped by a woman than by a man.

If he is slapped by a man, he feels the pain briefly. But if he is slapped by a woman, he will never forget the insult and the bad omen. For three years he will be exposed to bad luck just because of the impact of a tender palm on his cheek. Of course he will demand an elaborate public apology, and he will probably receive that apology since a woman will hardly find her arguments upheld by public approval for slapping a man. And so it was with the lady in this case.

The cook in question demanded that she make a public apology to all the servants on the summit. This she did, to the losing of her "face" and the regaining of her cook's "face." Had she reneged, all of the servants on the mountain would have packed their gear and trooped back to Chengdu. Unfortunately, this particular cook happened to be the head of the Chengdu Servants' Union and his word was law. Why, if she had balked, he could also have called out on strike every servant in Chengdu along with those on White Deer Summit. To make things worse, she couldn't even fire that cook and find another. Had she tried it, the second cook's life wouldn't have been worth two cents.

As it was, she got off quite easy and didn't have to make the usual apology of burning a pair of candles at the insulted man's home and setting off a bombardment of firecrackers to ward off the bad luck brought on by the slapping—all at the woman's expense. In this incident, we can see something of the sexual inequality in China. In principal, sexual inequality has been wiped out in China. But one doesn't have to search far to find it still reflected in a hundred and one different ways, especially in the remote rural areas.

Though I've painted a rather stormy picture of our summer with its basket of summer fruit, we didn't expect an easy time of it when we gladly volunteered for China. The spiritual side of the picture was a much brighter one. What a joy it was to fellowship with missionaries from other societies and to join with them in praying for a revival to start in our own hearts and then sweep out across the Chengdu Plain. From our vantage point on White Deer Summit, we could not look to the south across that plain without feeling the urge to pray for the inhabitants of that vast area still steeped in superstition and idolatry.

To the east and north of us, we could see higher and more rugged mountain ranges. Their jagged peaks had been chiseled from granite. As we looked at them, it wasn't hard to understand why many Chinese still believe some of them are sacred and make annual pilgrimages to their summits. These pilgrimages lead them to temples on every range, starting with 6,000 foot White Deer

"AND BEHOLD, THERE WAS A BASKET ..."

Summit and leading them, in turn, to mountains ranging up to 12,000 feet. Many times I would gaze out the window at 8,000 foot Tien Tai and long to follow the pilgrimage route to the top, but my bum leg and bed continually said, "No." I had to lie in that bed with my leg propped up while Lucille and others made the overnight trip. Looking from my bedroom window, I could see them make the descent into a narrow valley and start their climb up the neighboring mountain. Since I had to remain behind, the only thing I can do is let Lucille tell you about it:

> Because we wanted to have a closer look at one of these "sacred" mountains, we followed the pilgrims' trail up Tien Tai. On both ides of the path were cultivated spots. No place seemed too remote or steep for the inevitable corn patch with beans or squash winding round the stalks and potatoes occupying all other available ground. The mountain was covered with a large variety of wild flowers; and we soon found ourselves surrounded by the bright orange of the tiger lily, the deep purple of a bell-shaped flower, and the blue of the hydrangea.
>
> We passed many wayside shrines before we came to the first large temple on the pilgrimage route. Here we stopped for a cup of tea and watched a number of pilgrims reverently presenting their burning incense to huge and hideous-looking idols. After each offering, an old priest sounded a gong. After completing their worship at this temple, the pilgrims went on their way with baskets strapped to their backs filled with incense and paper money (purchased from the priests with good money) to present elsewhere on their pilgrimage.
>
> We followed them up a steep incline—some young and rather modern judging from their permanented hair, others with the long, antiquated queue, and others so old and feeble that we marveled at their ability to keep going. Seventy times they stopped along the way to worship "sacred" trees and burn incense at a huge rock, the worship of which supposedly removes pain.

At one place along the way, we met a company of armed men who gruffly told us that they were hunters. Later, we learned it was a robber band. Praise the Lord, they treated us with more respect than they did that party of some forty pilgrims who were behind us on the trail. Our followers were robbed of the money they were going to use to purchase more offerings for the gods. Can't say we felt too sorry for them. What difference did it make whether the robbers or the priests got the money? Both the former and the latter are "birds of a feather."

At the top of the mountain, we almost ran into a large, smiling Buddha surrounded by other images and a huge tiger which is revered as the king of the mountain. From there we climbed several high and difficult steps to the temple proper. Old women with bound feet were virtually crawling down them to bow before the idols we had just left behind.

We climbed still more steps and found numerous pilgrims eating, having fortunes told, or worshipping. Soon a gong sounded and all of the priests, about ten in number, donned simple robes and went into the main worship room where they knelt on their individual pillows and joined in chanting prayers borrowed from India.

Small temple boys with the nine holes of the priesthood already burned in their heads pounded the gongs and sang more lustily than their elders. After much chanting and seemingly meaningless movements, they burned paper money before an image, took it into the outer court, and thus the ceremony was ended. More paper money was used to start a fire in a large cauldron which was still being refueled when we retired to an upper room, but not to sleep, for firecrackers kept going off at frequent intervals until late in the night and the place was filled with loud talking.

The following day, many of the pilgrims started out for the next mountain some 10,000 feet high, but we returned to White Deer Summit more eager than ever that these people know the true God.

Our vision of lost souls was not just a local one, not one that merely encompassed the people of these nearer mountains and the Chengdu Plain. Far to the west we could see the snow-clad "Three Sisters" towering majestically at heights of over 20,000 feet and marking the geographical boundary of Tibet, not the political boundary established in 1939.

Nestled away in those mountains are countless Buddhist lamaseries or temples carrying on their sad program of forcing precious souls for whom Christ died to prostrate themselves before images of wood and stone and causing them to utter their one prayer of "O mani padmi hum" ("Thou Jewel of the Lotus") in a thousand and one different ways. That Jewel in the Lotus, of course, is Buddha.

Buddhists believe that Buddha sprouted out of a lotus blossom and that's why the idols of Buddha include such a blossom. We prayed for the day when the Lotus would wither away and "The Lily of the Valley" would start to bloom in the hearts of those tribespeople to the west. It was to these tribal areas that we had felt our call and every westward glance reminded us of this fact and made us long to move in that direction.

It was all well and good for us to sit on a mountain top and look westward, but the only way to get there was to tarry again in the plain until certification came from our language teachers and senior missionaries. So, having fully devoured our basket of summer fruit, we pulled stakes and returned to Chengdu where we continued our study of the language which was finally beginning to make some sense after all. I had begun to have some doubts. The Lord was good in quickening my mind to the task and showed great patience with me, but I still didn't feel "at home" in the language.

Although my time was well-occupied with language study, I still found time to do some witnessing. As far as actual speaking engagements were concerned, I was still limited mainly to teaching English Bible classes. Most of those who attended were more interested in hearing and learning English than they were in studying the Word. Nevertheless, I didn't miss the opportunity of saturating the entire lesson with the Gospel message, praying inwardly for the Spirit to touch the hearts of my listeners.

Many of the people in my class were students at West China Union University. Even though it was a Christian campus, many of the people on the campus were not Christians. Included among them were students, servants, gardeners, amahs, and other school employees. Most of them were Buddhists and their lives were controlled by a myriad of troubling and complex beliefs and superstitions. One of these superstitions came to have a particularly real and distressing meaning.

Death stalked the campus one day and claimed the life of a little girl, the daughter of a Chinese professor. Her body was recovered from an irrigation ditch into which she had fallen and drowned. The water was only about four feet deep. When I arrived at the scene shortly after they had taken her body out of the water, it was too late to attempt artificial respiration for she had already been in the water for about an hour. I was shocked to find several of the witnesses to this tragedy laughing. I was barely able to restrain myself from confronting them and condemning their callousness. Lee Lovegren later explained to me that laughing is a Chinese way of coping with tragedy and should not be considered an expression of callousness or disrespect.

The most tragic aspect of this sad event was that the girl could have easily been saved had it not been for the superstition of those who knew of her plight and refused to rescue her. Several people watched her drown in shallow water rather than help and thereby risk the possibility of someone in their own families meeting a similar fate. According to one of their beliefs, the rescue of a drowning person spells death by drowning for some member of the rescuer's family. To save a drowning person was to interfere with the claim of the river god to the victim. A successful rescuer would be criticized for saving a life that rightfully belonged to the river god and for preventing the victim from joining his ancestors in Buddhist paradise. In some cases, the rescuer would be obligated to support the rescued person for the rest of his earthly life. And so ... a little girl died. How I longed for the ability to reach the minds and souls of these people with the truth of God's Word, but my knowledge of the Chinese language still amounted to nothing more than baby talk. Even though my inability to make myself understood hindered my witnessing, I did have a number of opportunities to be of service in a musical way by playing my accordion. One of those opportunities came when I assisted in a four-day Youth for Christ Campaign conducted by Bob Pierce. Andrew Chi, an outstanding Chinese evangelist served as his interpreter. A number of young people

"AND BEHOLD, THERE WAS A BASKET ..." 103

realized the joy of salvation and many others rededicated their lives to Christ.

My old accordion had a workout at the three services which were conducted each day and provided the musical accompaniment for Bob's solos which were particularly memorable for the dramatic choreography of his body gestures. One of them was that very familiar little chorus "This Little Light of Mine" which suggested the theme for this series of meetings: "Let your light so shine before men, that they may see your good deeds and praise your Father in Heaven" (Matt. 5:16).

Another musical opportunity came when Frank Meller of the China Inland Mission asked me to assist him at a street meeting outside the C.I.M. Church. He had lost his wife and three children in that plane crash at Hankou in January. There we were, that dedicated servant of God with his trumpet and me with my accordion, standing out on the street "playing our heads off" to attract a crowd while personal workers moved through the throng giving out tracts and inviting them into the church for the evening service. It reminded me of my street meetings down in San Francisco's skid row.

My accordion also came in handy at services conducted by Gladys Aylward. A book (*The Small Woman*) and a movie (*The Inn of the Sixth Happiness*) tell of her work in China. The movie starred Ingrid Bergman. Unlike Bergman, Gladys was a very small woman. As Gladys and I walked along the street together and visited patients in the leprosarium, I could see the faces of the people beam as they recognized "The Small Woman" in her Chinese gown and cloth sandals. Her days as a charwoman in England were over when, for the sake of Christ, she went to China via the Siberian Railroad, adopted the Chinese way of life, and became a citizen of China. The people considered her one of them and were glad to hear her talk about her Savior. She had been rejected as a missionary candidate in England and was told that she was not qualified to be a missionary. Though men may try, providentially it is God who finally selects.

During these months, we sensed an anti-Western feeling rapidly taking hold of China. Contempt for the foreigner could be seen on the faces of many people, especially the young. Open threats against the foreigner and his belongings became more and more common. Thieves began to take advantage of the situation. We were warned to be on the lookout—or should I say "sniffout"—for the odor of incense. They told us that a common practice among thieves is to loot a residence while the occupants are under the influence of a sleep-producing incense. It didn't take us long to go on the "sniffout," for several houses within a radius of a quarter mile of ours had just been robbed.

We were also on the "listen-out," for another little custom in the brotherhood of thieves is to enter a house by imitating the scratching and pattering of a rat. Since our house was "rat-haven," we found ourselves doing nocturnal sitting-up exercises. But despite all our precautions, on one occasion thieves broke into our house by removing the glass in one of our door panels and shoving a small child through it. On another occasion, there was quite a bit of excitement around our house when Ralph Covell's dog paid the price of being a thief's barrier. He suffered the usual death by arsenic poisoning. Added efforts were made to keep things under cover and to keep the children away from strange food in our yard.

Satan was certainly trying every possible trick to discourage us. His plan to defeat us was the same for the plain "as for the western border."

Chapter 13

"AS FOR THE WESTERN BORDER"

"As for the western border, you shall have the Great Sea, that is, its coastline; this shall be your west border." (Num. 34:6)

As for the western border of China, this was the territory God had given us for our sphere of work. I believe that God had his hand in this selection just as much as he had his hand in pointing out to Moses the western border of Israel. In our situation, two provinces were of particular interest, Qinghai and Xikang. Originally, the major portion of these provinces were within the borders of Tibet. In 1939, the Chinese Nationalist Government shortened the boundaries of Tibet by creating these two new provinces. At the same time, Generalissimo Chiang Kai-shek sent out a call for missionaries to enter the area.

One of the missionaries to answer the Qinghai call was my friend Virgil Hook of the China Inland Mission. His work among the Tibetans of that area had borne much fruit, and I welcomed his invitation for me to see that work during the Chinese New Year holidays in February of 1948. Welcome, too, was his promise to escort me to the Butter Festival and Devil Dance at Kumbum Lamasery.

Thanks to the wife's permission and vacation from language school, I was able to accept Virgil's invitation. Anyone of sound mind would have listened to all the warnings against traveling during the New Year holidays. Traveling to the high steppes of Tibet in mid-winter with little in the way of heavy clothing was unthinkable. Happily enough, I was too excited to spend much time considering the practical aspects of such a venture and departed with a small twenty-pound pack filled with a Testament, one change of clothing, shaving gear, and a sleeping bag.

Flying in those days was not only relatively cheap, but also the only way of getting to certain places in China. Knowing this, I headed for the airport in a standing room only, rickety, Dodge truck (an American Army relic). There were forty-six people on that truck, most of whom were just going out to the airport to wave goodbye to their flying friends. After a rough ten-mile trip through a shower which must have made the rain gods proud, we reached the Chengdu air strip and shivered in the rain until our plane arrived some four hours later. It was not without a little nostalgia that I climbed into a plane filled with Stateside comforts—plush seats, uniform heat, stewardess, individual lighting and ventilation system, and even paper bags for those not accustomed to flying and subject to throwing up.

We landed in the city of Chungking with its usual canopy of fog and clouds after a one-hour flight. Sitting in the plush seats of the C-47, thousands of feet above the rice paddies and the suffering masses below made me feel somehat like the Psalmist's dove who could escape and soar above his problems. But the jolting ride in an undersized sedan chair from an island airport in the Yangtze River, past the poor overcrowded hovels and beggars that lined the path, and up seemingly unending flights of steps to the China Inland Mission brought me back with a start to a needy and suffering world.

After an evening of fun, food, and fellowship at the C.I.M., I tumbled into bed and slept the sleep of peace until I was rudely awakened by an alarm clock at 3:00 A.M. Fifteen minutes later, I was asleep on a bench in a freezing airline office waiting for a bus to take me to an airport north of town where planes bound for Xian in Shensi Province took off. Five and half hours later, I opened my eyes and looked into a sea of Chinese faces, all gazing intently at the sleeping foreigner with the "gao-bi-dze" (high nose).

I was right in the midst of ironing the kinks out of my body when a series of unearthly explosions shook the building. One moment later, the ticket agent was pushing me out the door and into the thing that was making all the noise. Some people actually had the nerve to call it a bus. Since the wooden benches on the inside of the bus were too close together, I managed by placing my pack on the seat and sitting on it in a semi-standing position, an act which my poor head regretted after getting underway. Once settled on that seat there was no hope of moving since people were pressing on every side.

My trip on that broken down piece of junk is never to be forgotten. I tremble every time I think of it. Our driver was one of those typical gasoline cowboys who delighted in throwing caution to the wind. He picked up speed in second gear for the first half mile and slammed into high as we approached a busy and crowded intersection. Certain we weren't going to make it, I let out a final yell and covered my eyes. When I opened them a few moments later, the bus was creeping up a steep grade and the cowboy was giving me a very curious look. Looking right back at him, I vowed if I ever got out of that insult to the automotive industry alive I'd never enter it again.

I'm convinced he knew what I was thinking and purposely set out to make my last trip with him one that I'd never forget. For two hours we skidded in the rain over slippery mountain roads and careened around horseshoe curves hardly wide enough for one vehicle let alone two. Cowboy raced around blind curves without so much as even a reflex effort to blow his horn. Only once did I open my eyes and that was only after the bus made a half spin and came to a sudden stop. It was at right angles to the road with its rear wheels just six inches from a yawning chasm below.

That was the final straw. The other passengers didn't seem to mind much and faithfully stuck with the ship. My faith, however, wasn't as great as theirs. Grabbing my pack, I crawled out over that solid mass of laughing humanity and hitch-hiked a ride to the field in another contraption.

After shivering on the airfield until four in the afternoon, we were told that something was wrong with the little thingumajig that controlled the pitch of our plane's propeller. Though company officials insisted that it was unimportant and urged the crew to take off, the American pilot, although appreciating his flight pay, told them in no uncertain terms that they could take off without him. He wasn't going to take off until he had a fifty-fifty chance of coming out alive. Apparently he was fed up with the company's system of equipping one plane by stripping another plane of its emergency or back-up equipment. Perhaps he was thinking of all those fatal crashes in the winter of 1946.

Worse than missing my flight was the realization that I'd have to take that bus from Hades back to Chungking. As I climbed aboard, cowboy gave me a leer that sent shivers down my spine. Suffice it to say, the trip back was just as bad as the trip out. Once back in town, I again vowed that I would never enter that bus again. But the next morning, I found myself again at the plane office at 3:30 A.M. And once again, after a five-hour wait, we stood in front of cowboy and his bus. Once again we defied death as cowboy skidded over the

same old road to the same old airport. Once again I repeated the same old vow about not risking my life in that bus again. And once again, after another all day wait, we learned that our flight had been postponed again. This time it was due to heavy snows to the north that blanketed the airport at Xian with six inches of snow.

Back in Chungking that night after clipping two rickshas and a hand cart, I decided to equip myself with some warmer clothing. The cheap pair of heavy trousers that I bought didn't look so good, but they filled the bill until six o'clock that night at which time they ripped from top to bottom while I was in the act of sitting down at the supper table. Fortunately, Esther Nelson, an associate of our mission, was in town and came to the rescue with a needle and thread.

The next morning, I was up at seven instead of three. I couldn't see any sense in spending four hours of the night sleeping on an

"AS FOR THE WESTERN BORDER"

office bench when I could just as well be sleeping on a good mattress. What difference did it make whether or not they asked us to be in the office before 3:30 A.M.? The bus never left until nine anyhow. Furthermore, I was usually the only one to show up at 3:30 A.M. The other passengers were continually showing up several hours later.

After a hearty breakfast, I headed for the office and still had an hour to wait after my arrival. By this time I had given up the practice of saying goodbye to my C.I.M. friends. It was now, "So long, I'll see you later." Cowboy must have had some premonition that we'd take off that day and did his double best to scare the life out of me on that last wild ride.

At three o'clock that afternoon we were just on the verge of heading back to Chungking when word came through that the Xian field was open. Our flight to the city of Nestorian Tablet fame lasted about two and a half hours and took us over one rugged snowcapped mountain range after another. I actually would have enjoyed the flight had it not been for the fact that our plane was without heat. At 8,000 feet, we found the temperature one degree below zero.

After a weekend stopover in Xian with Scandinavian Alliance missionaries who soon had me out on the streets preaching through an interpreter, I took off for Lanzhou in Gansu Province. There I spent a week huddling around fires on the China Inland Mission compound when not busy seeing the town. It was there that I caught my first view of the world's most fickle stream, the Huangho or Yellow River which is 2,900 miles long. It rises in Tibet and flows eastward to the Yellow Sea. The river is called "Yellow" because of the "yellow earth" which it holds in suspension as it travels its long course to the sea. Its flooding and frequent changes in course, along with the consequent incalculable loss of life and property, have given the river the name of "China's Sorrow." The ice on the river was four feet thick when I walked across it to the C.I.M. hospital on the other side. I was really impressed with the physical and spiritual healing ministry being done at the hospital, but I wasn't impressed by the sight that I saw there. Two American staff members who were somewhat overweight were sitting at a table heaped with food and drinking strawberry milkshakes. At least that's what I thought they were drinking until they offered me some out of a container. They told me it was Metrical, a brand new product from America which helped people lose weight. So far, they hadn't lost any weight, but they said it was just a matter of time. The drink had just reached the market place about the time of our departure from the States. You should have seen the look on their faces when I told them that Metrical was a meal in itself, containing all the proper vitamins and nutrients. In order to lose weight, they would have to discontinue all other foods.

I was surprised to learn that one part of the wall around the hospital compound was actually a part of the Great Wall of China which was built in feverish haste by Emperor Shih Huangdi as a rampart against the Tartars of the North. A million men, including thousands of criminals and prisoners of war, were forced to work on the wall until it was completed in 204 B.C. It stretches about 2500 miles from Gansu Province in the west to the eastern coast of the land. It's interesting to note that this was the only man-made object recognized by our astronauts in space.

The Great Wall played its part well until 1209 A.D. when it was crossed by the Mongol hordes under Genghis Kahn. It was his grandson, Kublai Khan, who in 1280 asked Nicolo and Maffeo Polo, father and uncle, respectively of Marco Polo, to go back to Italy and return with one hundred Christian missionaries to teach religion and the arts to his Tartars and to bring him some oil from the sacred lamp on the Holy Sepulcher at Jerusalem. The merchants waited for two years for the election of a Pope; but when their friend Gregory X was finally elevated, he was only able to send two Dominicans—two missionaries to win Asia!

They took the holy oil and young Marco Polo and headed eastward. It wasn't long before the two Dominicans turned back, thinking their mission useless because of turmoil in Armenia. But the three Polos, guarding their battered vessel of holy oil, pressed on. One can't help wondering what the results might have been had the Pope been able to send one hundred missionaries to China. Perhaps it might have been a Christian country today. When the Khan's request was not fulfilled, he turned to India for Buddhist teachers.

Marco Polo mentions in his diary the city of Xining in Qinghai Province. This was my destination after leaving Lanzhou. Xining is about 200 miles west of Lanzhou. Virgil Hook was all dressed up in Tibetan garb when he met my truck upon its arrival in the city. He soon had me peddling my way by bicycle to Kumbum Lamasery, about twenty miles southwest of Xining.

"AS FOR THE WESTERN BORDER"

A big surprise was in store for me when Virgil Hook ushered me into a Tibetan home near the lamasery and announced that it was our dwelling place for the next few days. The thing that horrified me was his comment that the custom in Tibet was for the husband to sleep elsewhere when male guests came to the house. The wife was to be turned over to the male guests for their pleasure. When I heard this, I was ready to run out of the house and head back to my wife and child.

Virgil pointed out that this custom was one of the biggest problems in Tibet. Syphilis and other venereal diseases were running rampant in the land. As we walked along the streets together, he showed me women lying in the streets, unable to move, because of these diseases and with nothing being done for them medically. They were simply left in the streets to die.

My panic was calmed when Virgil explained American customs to our Tibetan hosts. The husband was persuaded to stay at home. To a Tibetan, the turning down of another man's wife was a severe insult to the wife and the husband and might have resulted in a lethal duel. Though our hosts, devout Lamaists, went out of their way to make us feel at home, I'm afraid I squirmed a little at having to sleep on the kang with the old grandfather and grandson. During the cold winters, the Tibetans sleep on kangs, large brick stove affairs kindled from below with yak dung. As could be expected, because of the chill, I was frozen on one side and toasted on the other. This meant rolling over and over all night long, bumping into Virgil on one side and into the grandfather on the other. It wouldn't have been so bad sleeping with my new found friends were it not for the fact that other "bed-fellows" were present—bedbugs.

The unique experience of eating food with my hands was a real treat. The main course was "zamba" (barley-flour), big chunks of yak meat and butter, all mixed together by hand. Pieces of yak dung had accidentally fallen into it. As my hosts turned aside to serve us or talk to Virgil, I'd quickly pick out as many pieces of dung as I could and drop them on the floor where the dogs were waiting to gobble them up. Tea completed the meal.

Kumbum Lamasery is second only in importance to the lamasery in Lhasa. At the time, Kumbum boasted 4,000 priests and was the residence of the Panchen Lama, the spiritual leader of Tibet. The Dalai Lama, the political leader, was in Lhasa. The fame of Kumbum is wrapped up in the fact that it is the birthplace of Tsong Kaba, the "Martin Luther" of Tibetan Lamaism—founder of the predominant Yellow Sect. The Yellow or Reformed Sect might be considered the established church of Tibet.

The famous Butter Festival attracted pilgrims and worshippers from all parts of central Asia—Tibetans, Mongols, Chinese, and aboriginal people. All of the roads leading to the lamasery were packed with yak and camel trains, pilgrims prostrating themselves on the roads which were six inches deep with dust, merchants with their wares, Mongol princes with their retinue of princesses and many other folk.

On the day preceding the Butter Festival, a performance called the "Devil Dance" was held. Not wanting to miss a thing, we took our places early to watch this spectacle, every phase of it having some peculiar religious significance. Our interest was soon captured by the central figure of the dance, the God of Sickness and Death, who wore an enormous bull's head mask of black and gold with horrible protruding eyes and huge black horns. With the scepter of death in his right hand, the fearsome god appeared on the steps of the chanting hall and instilled fear into the hearts of his Tibetan audience. Later he was joined in the dance by his retinue of demons, the Bowa.

As the God of Sickness and Death entered the arena, many worshippers tried to rush to him for healing instead of waiting for him to approach them on the sidelines, but husky lama guards with big leather whips drove them back. While all of this was going on, and before Virgil could grab me, I ran out into the center of the arena and took pictures of the "god" as he approached. The poor guards didn't know what to do with this strange foreigner with the camera, so they left me alone. How stupid of me to desecrate this ritual.

The person who should have been whipped was Dan Carr. The least I could have done was to show a little tolerance for this very important religious observance. What would we do if a bunch of Tibetans broke into one of our churches in America and began to desecrate the sanctuary? We watched hundreds of pilgrims bowing down before this grotesque figure as he approached them on the sidelines. They offered him salutation scarves in the hope that this act would save them from sickness and death. At sundown on the day of the festival, dozens of idols were placed at intervals on the lamasery grounds. Some were small and others gigantic, reaching up over ten or fifteen feet. All of these idols represented some god or goddess and varied little in form except in the hundreds of decorations surrounding them—animals of all kinds, dragons, scenes from hell and paradise, flowers, castles, lamaseries and numerous other miniature figures.

The wonder of it all was that these idols and other figures were all moulded out of yak butter. For sheer ingenuity, these figures moulded by Tibetan hands and painted in the brightest of hues were unrivalled. The sight of them would have been most beautiful were it not for the fact that thousands of pilgrims fanatically bowed down before them. How zealous they were! We couldn't help but ask ourselves the question, "If the worshippers of a dead Buddha are so sincere, how much more fervent should we be in our worship of a living Savior?"

How helpless we felt in the midst of all the festivities. The most Virgil could do was to give a hurried word of testimony here and there; and the most I could do, not being able to speak the language, was to help distribute several thousand tracts. But certainly God blesses such efforts.

Our Kumbum visit culminated in a personal audience with the Panchen Lama himself, a mere child of ten yet revered by millions. Several times we had watched him being carried through the temple grounds with his train of attendants and imagined him to be a cold and sullen lad. But in the seclusion of his own private quarters, we found him to be a poor bewildered little fellow who probably would have traded all of his pomp and glory for the fun and companionship of those his own age. We presented our salutation scarves to him as he sat upon a "sacred" chair. Forgetting all about protocol and revealing my stupidity, I handed my camera to Virgil and had him take a picture of me standing at the boy's side. There I was towering over him when I probably should have been sitting at the Panchen Lama's feet.

Much more could be said about the Panchen Lama and Kumbum with its many idols of butter, silver, and gold, but enough has been mentioned to make us want to cry out with the Psalmist again: "The idols of the nations are but silver and gold, the work of man's hands." (Psa. 135:15) After having my eyes opened to the desperate spiritual need on the northern part of the western border, it came time for me to head back to Chengdu and prepare myself for my first look at the southern part of this border. The first part of my trip back was made in the back of a beaten up old truck jammed with Tibetans. An old Tibetan man sat right in front of me and stared into my face as he counted his "rosary" of one hundred and nine beads. Each bead called for the saying of the one Tibetan prayer, "O Mani Padmi Hum." The more times it was repeated, the more blessings were received.

My eyes were hypnotically fixed on those beads hour after hour, and my nostrils were filled with the awful stench of rancid butter. In the winter, the Tibetans constantly plaster their bodies with yak butter in order to protect themselves against the cold. Furthermore, it is against their religion to bathe. Only twice on that twelve hour trip did I find relief from the congestion. Once when a large camel train bumped our truck, causing the passengers to jump out in fear. The other time was when somebody called for a "pit stop." Some of the people had to relieve themselves. Out of the truck they jumped, men and women alike. There they squatted side by side as I crawled in embarrassment to some bushes alongside the road.

How those passengers got back into the truck again each time and assumed their original positions was beyond me. All I know is that I found myself looking again into the face of the old man with the beads and hearing him say, "O Mani Padmi Hum." For twelve straight hours, the tune was the same, "O Mani Padmi Hum." When I finally rolled out of that truck at the end of the first stage of my journey home, I found myself walking around the streets of the town saying over and over again in my mind, "O Mani Padmi Hum." And when I tried to sleep that night in a primitive little inn, I found the same words filling my mind, "O Mani Padmi Hum. O Mani Padmi Hum. O Mani Padmi Hum."

Back in Lanzhou again, I caught a truck filled with postage sacks and passengers going south to Chengdu. We followed the very famous highway ("washboard" road) known as the "Road of the Golden Ox." According to legend, this road was built at great expense so the wild oxen in the mountains might be captured. The people believed their fodder was changed into gold. This horrible road took us over Wudong Pass at the western end of the Jiuling Mountains and on to the Sichuan Plain.

As we slowly made our way up the grade in second gear, a rattletrap bus full of freight and passengers came roaring down the hill like the "Four Horsemen of the Apocalypse" and almost sideswiped us—no chains, no tread on the tires, and probably no brakes. Everybody in the bus smiled and waved as it shot by us and skidded around the next curve which hung over a precipice 1,000 feet high. In addition to all this, it began to rain. The rain soon turned into a deluge and this missionary soon began to wonder if he was going to end up in just another nameless grave along the road.

I must confess that I did not lose my appetite along the way. Were it not for the peanuts that we bought from venders on the road, I probably would have starved to death. No wonder the Chinese call peanuts the "Longevity Fruit." What a relief it was when our truck stopped at a little inn where we would spend the night. Naturally, I was very hungry and relishing a good meal. In no time at all, I was sitting at a roadside stand and ordering food.

Since I was still not able to read a Chinese menu, I had to leave the choice of food to the waiter who was also the cook. To tell the truth, the place didn't even have a menu. The waiter/cook had a towel wrapped around his waist. A guest had just left the table where I was seated and his dirty dishes were in front of me. The waiter took his towel, wiped the sweat from his brow, and then used the same towel to wipe the dirty dishes on my table. Who was I to complain about his way of doing things? After all, he didn't complain about my disgusting Western habit of blowing my nose and then putting the filthy handkerchief into my pocket.

I soon found a steaming bowl of rice topped by strips of delicious looking meat in front of me. I really enjoyed the food and complemented the cook. I also asked him about the ingredients, hoping that my wife would be able to duplicate the dish. I was particularly anxious for him to identify the meat. Though there were many words in the Chinese language that I did not know, there were two very common words that I did know. These words that flowed calmly and unmistakably from the lips of this smiling and proud cook were, "Rat meat." Immediately my stomach revolted and I made a hasty retreat and deposited what food I had eaten in a corner from whence it had probably come.

My recovery from dinner was hastened by the diverting of my attention to the peculiar antics of the driver of our truck. I saw him drain and remove the truck's radiator and carry it into the inn. Why? Simple enough. He didn't want it to freeze overnight. The next morning, I watched him replace the radiator and then slide a large pan of red hot charcoal under the engine in order to thaw it out. I must have broken all Olympic records as I sought protection behind a distant tree. This procedure became the daily routine until we finally crossed Wudong Pass and made our way down to Chengdu on the plain.

My journey to Tibet was more than just a passing interest. It was my first real sight of the spiritual need among the tribal people to the west. It challenged me to pray more fervently that God would help me meet this need among the cousins of the Tibetans, the Nosu, who lived to the south of them in Xikang Province. The trip also encouraged me to give more attention to my language study in Chengdu in order that I might be fully equipped to meet the overwhelming need among the tribes.

It was good to be back in Chengdu again with Lucille and Danny and the rest of our missionary family. And it was good to get back to the study of the language and back to the job of putting that language to use by witnessing on the streets.

One thing was certain, we never lacked for an audience to preach to in China. We had to do little more than stoop down and tie our shoelaces to draw a crowd. In fact, we didn't have to go to that much trouble. We could simply stand on a street corner and within five minutes there would be a crowd of people surrounding us. It was amazing! But how we looked forward to the day when they would crowd around us, not to listen to our peculiar speech, but to hear of the One who could bring light to their dark world.

I often remember that little orphan boy who was playing the organ at the Chengdu School for the Blind. He was totally blind and only ten years of age, but he virtually made that organ speak out the words of the hymn "The night is dark, and I am far from home." The words of that song certainly reflected the spiritual darkness of China. Among those suffering in the darkness were the people we were anxious to reach, the Nosu tribespeople to the southwest in Xikang Province where, too, "the harvest is plentiful, but the laborers are few."

Chapter 14

"THE HARVEST IS PLENTIFUL, BUT THE LABORERS ARE FEW"

"And He was saying to them, 'The harvest is plentiful, but the laborers are few; therefore beseech the Lord of the harvest to send out laborers into His harvest.'" (Luke 10:2)

It's interesting to note how the Lord often used rural life to illustrate His spiritual teachings. He looked upon the Samaritans as a ripe harvest ready to be gathered in but found those who were willing to reach them discouragingly few. The shortage of laborers has continued to be the history of Missions from Christ's time to today. It was certainly true in our case as we finished our language study in Chengdu and made ready to start our work in that great harvest field on the western border of China.

The field of work mapped out for us (see front of book) was the Anning Valley which was in the great loop of the Yangtze River. The Valley's length stretched over one hundred miles from north to south. Its width was less than five miles on the average. It was bordered on the north by the River of Silver Sands and on the south by the River of Golden Sands which leads into the Yangtze River (the River of Gold). To the east was the Daliangshan (the Great Cold Mountains) with peaks reaching up to 19,000 feet. To the west were other very high mountains which made up the eastern edge of the Himalayas. One peak, Minya Gonka, rose to a height of some 25,000 feet.

The Anning Valley, averaging about a mile above sea level, is part of the route that Marco Polo, Kublai Khan, and many other famous travelers have followed—even Mao Zedong on his famous "Long March" of 1934-1935. The Chinese, who numbered about 800,000 at the time of our arrival, lived in the valley and along the principal roads. The Nosu tribespeople, who numbered about 1,500,000, occupied the mountains. The Christian witness among these two groups was practically non-existent.

"ME? A MISSIONARY?"

On April 2, 1948, our little band of missionaries boarded the "St. Paul" (the Lutheran Mission plane—a converted U.S. Army C-47) and said goodbye to Chengdu. Though we had been anticipating the plane's arrival for several weeks that still didn't prevent the mad rush of last minute packing—a rush that hindered us from taking full advantage of the meetings sponsored by Youth for Christ with Dawson Trotman of the Navigators organization. I was very much involved in the work of the Navigators when I was a Navy chaplain in Jacksonville, Florida. I first met Dawson at his headquarters in Pasadena, California, and volunteered to open a Navigators' ministry among service men and women in the Jacksonville area. We were delighted that he could be in Chengdu to ground key Christians in the Word, and certainly the Lord blessed the seed that was sown. It was great to see "Daws" again and fellowship with him in our home. But now it was time to "Go!"

Within the space of a few hours we were speedily transported to a part of China about one hundred years behind the rest of China and quite different from the cultural center of Chengdu. It would have taken several weeks to travel over the bandit-infested mountain roads to our new home in the Anning Valley. This home was nothing compared to our home on the campus of West China Union University. It was located on a hill in the town of Xichang and consisted of four adobe buildings surrounded by a wall. Ceilings were lacking, and the windows were made out of oiled rice paper since glass was a rare commodity in that part of China. A common outhouse was located right in the middle of the compound and water was carried in daily by coolies.

The house that we lived in had formerly been used as a tobacco drying shed. It was dark and dingy and black stains were still on the walls when we moved in. Until we had time to make the necessary renovations, we had to share it with some mighty big rats. Our first night was a nightmare. Though we had covered our beds with mosquito netting, we still had to do a lot of scratching. I turned on my flashlight to attack some mosquitoes that had gotten inside of the net only to quickly lose my interest in those miserable mosquitoes when I noticed the net swarming with bedbugs.

What a relief it was to hop out of bed the next morning and take a look around the town. There was a real contrast between the Chinese here and those on the Chengdu Plain. As we walked along the streets with small adobe buildings and open shops, we were depressed by the physical appearance of the people with their ragged clothing. Many of them were stunted in growth (cretins) because of a lack of iodine in the drinking water. Government health officials estimated at that time that over 75% of the people had visible goiters, some immense. It was also estimated that over 60% of the people here and in the surrounding villages were opium addicts. Mothers gave it to their children in order to pacify them.

Work among the Chinese in Xichang was quite a challenge for there were so very few who knew Christ. Most of the people were hearing the Gospel story for the first time. Truly they were as sheep without a shepherd, yet they seemed most willing to pack our little street chapel to hear our senior missionaries and national workers tell the story of the True Shepherd. The rest of us were also anxious to tell that story, but we still hadn't adequately mastered the tool that would make it possible—the language.

Two months after our arrival came a day that I'll never forget. The morning of June 7, 1948, was the day our second child, James Randolph, decided to make his appearance. I was particularly happy since it was my first opportunity to prove myself during the birth and "cradle" period. I was overseas in the Philippines when Dan, Junior, was born and didn't see him until many months later when I returned to the States after the war.

This "proving" period was definitely not an easy one. Unfortunately, Jimmy decided to arrive several weeks sooner than expected and we were not quite ready to receive him. Our house was still being renovated. A young Chinese midwife had promised to deliver the baby. However, when I dashed to her home at two o'clock in the morning, she was frightened nigh unto death and refused to accompany me. She said she had only delivered a few babies and didn't feel qualified. I told her that she was far more qualified than I. After much begging on my part, she finally agreed to go with me.

The first thing she asked for when she arrived at Lucille's side was hot water and something hard to put on the mattress. The only hard thing I could think of was our new outhouse door. The outhouse was situated right in the middle of our compound with all the missionary homes surrounding it. Not having any modern hardware such as hinges, local carpenters had attached the door to the house with wooden dowls. All one had to do to remove the door was to lift it off its dowls. That's exactly what I did, despite the fact that Ralph Covell just happened to be using the privy at the time. He let out a terrible scream and cried, "Where are you going with that door?" I quickly replied, "Oh, quiet down. I need it more than you do!" and ran to our home with the door.

All of the others on the compound heard the racket and rushed to our house. In that crowd were the other missionaries and their children, amahs, coolies, cooks and their families, cats, dogs, and everything else that could walk. Even the neighbors had climbed up on the walls to find out the source of that great hullabaloo. In no time at all, Lucille was on the door gritting her teeth in pain. Since we had no medicine to ease her pain, not even an aspirin tablet, I told her to bite on my hand, and bite she did. Between contractions, she calmly told me that she was going to die—no crying, no apparent fear, just a calm matter of fact declaration, "Dan, I'm going to die." My only response was, "Bite a little harder, Honey!"

What a relief it was when young Jim arrived. That sense of relief soon disappeared when the midwife tried to rush things by pulling on the afterbirth. Even I knew this was a dangerous thing to do, so I grabbed her arm and told her to stop. Once the ordeal was over, I slumped into a chair and nursed my well-chewed hand. Irene Simpson was really a jewel for helping with the delivery and bearing the heaviest load in caring for the newest arrival.

Several weeks after Jim's birth, I was ready for a much needed rest. That rest consisted of joining Ralph Covell on a thirty-mile walk to a Nosu village high up in the mountains to the west. Our visit gave us a real insight into tribal life and left us both with an anxious desire to give these tribal people the Gospel, but there were still many more months of language study and training in Xichang ahead of us before we could work among the tribes.

Our little street chapel in Xichang bustled with activity with Sunday School and two evangelistic services on Sunday, a women's meeting on Tuesday afternoon, children's meetings in the afternoon and prayer meeting on Wednesday night, another evangelistic service on Thursday night, Chinese Bible Class on Friday, and an English Bible Class Saturday night. A program of visitation was also initiated to follow up the contacts made in our chapel services.

After many months of faithful witnessing by both national workers and missionaries, there was a gathering in of our first fruits and we were all on "shouting ground." One of these first fruits was an elderly lady who, while making her way to a sacred mountain near Xichang, happened to wander into our little street chapel and soon lost all her desire to continue her pilgrimage. Why? One of our new converts led her to the Lord. Then there was Mrs. Yang who had very bad eyes. The Great Physician healed her physical as well as her spiritual eyes. In every testimony meeting she would tell about this miracle which took place in her life. Mrs. Yang was also instrumental in her daughter as well as her daughter-in-law finding the Lord.

Chiang Chung Ch'i, our cook's son, also had his spiritual eyes opened wide as well as Mr. Lo, a young man in his thirties who worked for a local distillery. He was delivering whiskey to his customers when he saw a big crowd outside our chapel. His curiosity led him into the building where he found something better to quench his thirst—the "Living Water." Another young man, Mr. Li, tasted this water and was determined to offer it to others. He showed a real interest in becoming a minister of the Gospel.

Another one to drink of the "Living Water" was Mrs. Yang who had been married when she was just a child. Child-brides were common in that day. Her parents had chosen a husband for her and arranged the marriage with his parents. Soon after giving birth to her first child, her husband died and her drunken father who was a gambler with a terrible temper ordered her to return to his home. Life had lost all meaning for her and she was on the verge of suicide when one of our new converts brought her to the chapel where she accepted Christ as her Savior and Lord.

Our first fruits increased in number and soon began to witness to their loved ones and friends. The husband of one of these new Christians came under deep conviction of sin in his home. He was in such a sad plight that he couldn't sleep at night and finally begged his wife and daughter and granddaughter—all new converts—to pray for him.

The Chinese New Year holiday season was a busy one as we led our new converts out into the surrounding villages where they gave their testimonies. We foreigners with our very "high noses" (the Chinese term for foreigners) attracted the crowds. I contributed my "high nose" and loud accordion to the cause. This was the first time these people had ever heard such a strange musical instrument. This was also the first time they had ever heard the Gospel. Our hearts were thrilled to hear our converts testify.

Another one of our first fruits was Miss Chu, a woman forty years of age. For years she had thirsted for peace of heart, a thirst which led her into many years of special Buddhist training and caused her to keep the vegetarian vow for eighteen long years. Slowly her health began to fail and finally it came to the place where her family began making preparations for her funeral. They expected her to die at any moment. It was just about this time that she heard sounds coming from our chapel which was located right next to her home. She left her home, staggered into the chapel, and listened to a very important message given by the Great Physician himself:

> "And Jesus answered and said to them, 'It is not those who are well who need a physician, but those who are sick. I have not come to call righteous men but sinners to repentance'" (Luke 5:31,32).

"THE HARVEST IS PLENTIFUL ..."

Half-believing that Christ could heal her body as well as her soul, she made her way home feeling much happier. Well, that was just the first of her many visits. In the weeks that followed she did become a very earnest inquirer despite the persecution of her own family. Three times they called a Buddhist priest to deal with her and three times she thought her family or the priest had tried to poison her, for each visit caused her to suffer nausea, dizziness, and bodily pain.

Providentially, our national woman evangelist, Miss Hu Gaihsiang, happened to show up immediately after each of her sessions with the priest. Prayer and a rich feasting on the Word soon brought relief to her body and finally led to her drinking that cup of Living Water to the last drop. In Christ she found both healing of body and soul. So sincere was this woman in her new found faith that she not only became one of our finest workers but also refused to have any part in family preparations for the Buddhist funeral of her mother who had died six months earlier. For six months the family had waited for a lucky day to bury her. When the lucky day finally arrived, Miss Chu was not to be found in the funeral train. Where was she? Out on the streets preaching the Gospel.

Of course this meant increased persecution on the part of her family. They even tried to stop her from being baptized. But again God's providence was on her side, for I was able to lead her through the waters of baptism before the arrival of her family. They were three minutes too late. I still shiver every time I think of that baptismal service. It took place in a pond on our compound in the middle of winter on January 9, 1949. Despite Lee Lovegren's attempt to heat the water with large metal pots of hot charcoal floating on the water (all the heat went up), I was hardly able to feel my lower extremities for several days after the baptismal service.

Unfortunately, my frozen legs were not my only problem. Dr. James Broomhall, a medical missionary with the China Inland Mission and stationed in our area, discovered that "I, Daniel, was exhausted and sick."

"THE HARVEST IS PLENTIFUL ..."

"ME? A MISSIONARY?"

Chapter 15

"I, DANIEL, WAS EXHAUSTED AND SICK"

"Then I, Daniel, was exhausted and sick for days ..." (Daniel 8:27a)

The prophet Daniel had every reason to be exhausted and sick after his vision of the final Antichrist foreshadowed in an obscure but pretentious Greek ruler, Antiochus Epiphanes IV, who tried to stamp out the Jewish religion during the second century before Christ. The satanic power that possessed Antiochus is the same power that will possess the Antichrist in the last day and is hard at work today. It certainly was hard at work on our field in West China when our first fruits were being gathered in. It was determined to destroy all that the Lord had been doing in our valley, even if it meant bringing sickness upon His servants.

A number of our missionaries were suffering from one sickness or another. Malaria, typhus, typhoid, meningitis and dysentery were very common in this corner of China. I was unable to check recurring attacks of amoebic dysentery and my weight dropped from 210 pounds to 168 within the space of three months. I was also plagued with a chronic cough. Several doctors in West China had given various diagnoses: chronic bronchitis, chronic bronchiectasis, etc. All of these doctors traced the trouble to my chest, but their prescriptions didn't seem to remedy the condition.

When Elwin and Becky Stafford and their children were forced to leave the field because of sickness in the family, I was asked to fly with them on the *Saint Paul* to Shanghai and see them off on a steamer bound for the States. Our missionaries decided that I should be the one to accompany them since I could also take advantage of medical treatment in Shanghai. The flight took place in April of 1949.

After waving "goodbye" to the Staffords as they boarded their ship for America, I entered the China Inland Mission Nursing Home under the care of Dr. Paul Adolph. The dysentery was soon brought under control, but not the cough. After a month of treatment, 10 X-rays with and without lipiodol and barium, 108 penicillin shots, 528 pills, a violent reaction to the penicillin, and 16 adrenalin shots, the good doctor finally traced my trouble back to a tonsilectomy I had undergone several years before. He recommended a sympathectomy and sent me back to my old stamping grounds, the Country Hospital.

After three months of debate by the three specialists on my case, they finally decided to dissect and interrupt my superior laryngeal nerve, the one causing all the trouble. The chief surgeon from England was "licking his chops" and anxious to further his reputation by being the first one in medical history (so he said) to block the superior laryngeal nerve. This would probably win a few pages in the British Medical Journal, *The Lancet*.

On the other hand, the old American eye, ear, nose, and throat specialist in charge wasn't too anxious to lose his reputation by risking the possibility of destroying the motor nerves controlling my voice. After all, I was a minister and what good is a minister without a voice. I didn't relish the idea of losing my voice even though some might have considered it a blessing. The American chest specialist cast his tie-breaker vote with the English surgeon and I was readied for the scalpel and medical history.

The big day finally arrived. Textbooks were set up on stands and everything was in readiness as I was wheeled into the operating room. In short order the novocain needle was working its way into the pack of nerves just below my right ear. But what was intended to be a very simple local anesthetic turned out to be a spinal anesthetic from the neck down. The almost impossible had happened when the needle went right through and hit the cervical nerve. I was paralyzed from the neck down.

At first, the doctors were at a loss as to what had happened and wouldn't believe me when I told them that I couldn't breathe. They told me to relax and not worry. Finally, when there was no more breath left in me to do any talking and when it looked to me as though I were heading for "the other side," I decided to leave it all in the hands of the Lord. Actually, it was a very peaceful experience. I could see a long corridor with a great light at the end of it. There was no pain. I just couldn't breathe. A few seconds later, one of the doctors frantically began to give me artificial respiration. Then I passed out. Some time later, as I was being wheeled out of the operating room, I regained consciousness long enough to ask the nurse pushing me, "Where are you taking me?" Then I passed out again. I came to again for a few seconds and saw a cloud of faces hovering over me, heard somebody say, "Pulse, five," and then drifted back to dreamland. Later still, I woke up again and saw a wall of oxygen tanks around me and heard a nurse repeating over and over again, "Wake up, Dan!" My reply, before blacking out again, was, "Leave me alone. I want to sleep."

Several hours later I heard the "box-score" from the old specialist. He told me that I had probably received the highest spinal anesthetic in medical history and lived to tell the story. He told me that he had checked back over numerous medical records and could only find one other case like mine. Unfortunately, the patient died. He also told me that the chief surgeon was feeling a little "under the weather." In fact, he didn't show up for three days. Apparently my pulse had stopped. The doctors took turns giving me artificial respiration while others made vain attempts to borrow a pulmotor from other hospitals. Oxygen and five potent heart stimulants were administered along with a last desperate shot of adrenalin, but

nothing revived me. They finally gave up and were in the process of wheeling me to the morgue when something wonderful happened. The Lord stepped up to the plate, clouted the ball clean over the center field fence, and drove me in. The doctors called it "luck." But I knew it was a miracle and shared with them the truth of a Physician far greater than they.

Needless to say, I was not operated on that day. Several days later, after the surgeon had regained his nerve, everything went along fine. After three hours of feeling their way through my neck, pausing frequently to check the text books, and hearing the old specialist saying over and over again, "Steady, steady, steady," they finally found the nerve and dissected it. Then came an awful week of waiting to see if I could "toot my horn." It finally tooted and all was well. The spasmodic coughs were gone. I felt like a new man and Satan was foiled again.

Another weapon Satan used to drive us from our field of work was the Chinese Communists. Before flying to Shanghai, I had learned that the American Consulate had advised our mission society to make immediate plans for the evacuation of its missionaries if they were not ready to live under possibly hazardous conditions. A number of missionaries from other societies had already left China and were heading back to their native lands.

Soon after my arrival in Shanghai, the city was surrounded by Communist troops. I rode out the "Battle of Shanghai" on my bed in the Country Hospital. For several weeks we were lulled to sleep by the pounding of heavy artillery at the outskirts of the city. Finally, one morning about three o'clock, the static report of machine-gun fire on the streets outside told us that "liberation" was near. At first we thought the fighting had moved on to the compound itself. Later we learned that it had passed down the street in front of the hospital and a great "battle" took place at a nearby intersection. In fact, it got so "hot" that both sides, thinking that somebody might actually get hurt, decided to push on toward the center of town.

A few hours later we found ourselves gloriously "liberated." Several months of "nuisance bombings" by Nationalist planes followed. One tense moment came when four aerial bombs hit the Bubbling Well Cemetery about a block away. It sounded as though they had dropped in our back yard and the whole hospital trembled.

"I, DANIEL, WAS EXHAUSTED AND SICK"

Fortunately those bombs couldn't have hit a better spot and received no protest from the tombstones.

Breaking all the rules of international warfare, the Communists placed antiaircraft guns on top of our hospital building, making the place a prime target. This caused the planes, understandably, to ignore the large red cross covering the top of the structure. Though I mounted a wheelchair and traveled to the roof of the building by elevator to loudly remind the gunners of the rules of international warfare, the gun emplacements remained and blasted away at the planes flying overhead. A number of troops in the compound of the hospital tried to further impress the patients and staff by firing their little hand guns at planes flying at altitudes over 10,000 feet. Well, so much for pre and post liberation.

Along with my liberation by the Communists was my liberation from the Country Hospital and the beginning of my attempts to return to my family and work in West China. Since there was no way out of Shanghai at the time, I was asked to take over as organist at the Free Christian Church during the month of August. This I was ready to do when calamity struck again. While trying to teach some Australian missionaries how to play American football on the China Inland Mission compound, I abruptly ended the lesson and suffered real loss of "face" by rupturing the supra-spinatus tendon in my left shoulder. So, only ten days after leaving the Country Hospital, I returned to have my left arm placed in a plaster cast pointing straight up to the sky. I had just finished three and a half months in the hospital, and now I had to haul around a twenty-pound plaster "strait jacket" for three and a half more months. It was just about this time, too, that one of the worst typhoons in the history of Shanghai hit the town and kept us marooned for several days. What was going to happen next? By this time, I was beginning to think that the Lord was either punishing me for something or trying to make a Job out of me; but, unlike Job, a host of friends were praying for me and that made all the difference in the world.

After more than thirty trips to the proper government office, I was finally granted an exit visa. Now all I needed was a ship or plane. This was provided for when an American ship, the *General Gordon*, was allowed to pass through the Nationalist blockade at the mouth of the Yangtze River. I secured passage on it but soon struck another snag. The *Gordon* was to sail in three days for the British colony of Hong Kong and I was without a temporary Hong Kong visa. I stood and watched the ship sail off without me after numerous telephone calls and telegrams failed to produce the necessary visa in time.

A few days later an American freighter, the *Flying Clipper*, ran the Nationalist blockade and arrived in Shanghai. I arranged passage on it. However, my Hong Kong visa had still not been approved when it came time for the ship to sail. Providentially, bad weather delayed the ship a day and it was during this delay that my visa to Hong Kong finally came through. I joined the other passengers at the dock only to have the boarding delayed when several Nationalist planes came in to bomb the ship because it had run their blockade. So we all made a dash for cover. Fortunately, the bombs missed their target and we were finally able to go aboard. My role was now to change from a Job to a Jonah.

Off we went on the *Flying Clipper* only to be stopped at the mouth of the Yangtze by three Nationalist gunboats. One of them was the old U.S. destroyer *Thomas* that had been turned over to Generalissimo Chiang's navy. When we tried to make a run for international waters, the boats threatened to fire. Naturally, the captain of our ship decided to stop. To make things worse, a storm was gathering and the ship's fathometer showed only seven feet of water under the keel. Still we had to sit there for two days wondering what was going to happen next? Part of the problem involved the matter of "face" on the part of our captors. They had lost it when the ship had slipped through their blockade and entered a Communist port. Now they were intent on regaining "face." Another part of the problem had to do with the fact that our ship was laden down with Communist cargo bound for Hong Kong. This seemed to be the main bone of contention. The Nationalist Navy notified our captain that we could proceed to Hong Kong if we dumped our cargo overboard. This our captain refused to do.

On the third day, a British warship appeared on the horizon. Unfortunately, Admiral Horatio Nelson was not commanding that particular ship. We appealed to it for help but only condolences were forthcoming. Having no appetite for getting mixed up in a serious international incident, it stayed out in international waters. It was then that the British passengers aboard our ship began to fume. An urgent appeal made to the American Navy at Okinawa received a

"I, DANIEL, WAS EXHAUSTED AND SICK" 139

tactful response expressing deepest sympathy over our precarious position. Now the American passengers, too, began to fume.

Things got so bad that our captors finally had to let us move. It was either that or captor and captive ending up aground. The water was just too shallow. The order finally came for us to follow the gunboats to the Zhoushan Archipelago. Several hours later we dropped anchor in Chou-shan Bay not far from the city of Qinghai. At that time, the Communists were waging quite a battle for the island and the flashes and report of heavy artillery could be seen and heard to the west. This was our "haven of rest" for the next two weeks.

Our best source of entertainment was listening to the daily news reports over the radio. While the announcer was telling the world about the critical food shortage on our ship and the possibility of the crew and passengers starving to death, we were feasting on juicy prime steaks, fried chicken, mashed potatoes floating in butter and gravy, along with plenty of other good food to last a month. My only complaint was that I still had that heavy cast on my arm and fellow passengers had to cut my steaks for me.

Another thing that brought a laugh was a radio message from the shipowners in the United States ordering the captain to secure the passengers below and make a run for international waters. There we were surrounded by four gunboats without a chance in the world of getting away and the word comes through for us to make a run for it. The poor captain had an awful time trying to keep from laughing out loud. How did we finally get away? Let me sum it up in a bit of doggerel:

Our stubborn captain stood on the bridge
at dawn's early light
When the Chinese Navy, roused from sleep,
signalled across the bight:
"There's a bit of a fuss a-brewin' in the hills
down Qinghai way.
The Reds have paid us a visit, and it looks
as though they'll stay;

140 "ME? A MISSIONARY?"

*So with compliments and regrets, sir, and whether we're
right or wrong,
You may take your passengers and cargo, too, forthwith
to far Hong Kong!"*

Praise the Lord! The long ordeal was over and I was finally on my way to Hong Kong. I arrived there on a Monday afternoon and found the Lutherans readying their plane for a flight to Chungking on Tuesday with a load of missionaries and then on to Xichang on Wednesday with a load of freight. I squeezed my way aboard and soon found myself stepping out of the plane in Xichang into Lucille's arms, a mighty pleasant sight after an absence of seven months. For many long months we were unable to correspond with each other. Neither of us knew whether the other was dead or alive.

"I, DANIEL, WAS EXHAUSTED AND SICK"

I learned later that while my wife and our other missionaries in Xichang were praying that God might lead me safely back to the field, Mrs. Chiang—our devout Christian amah and Bible woman—was asking the Lord to provide a special plane for me in Hong Kong. The Lord certainly answered her prayers in a wonderful way, and He answered my prayers in the same way. He was still doing a great work of healing in my body. It wasn't long before Lucille grabbed a saw and removed my cast without sawing my arm off. "Then I got up again and carried on the King's business."

"ME? A MISSIONARY?"

Chapter 16

"THEN I GOT UP AGAIN AND CARRIED ON THE KING'S BUSINESS"

> *"... Then I got up again and carried on the King's business; but I was astounded at the vision, and there was none to explain it."* (Daniel 8:27)

As the old saying goes, "You can't keep a good man down." So it was in the case of the Prophet Daniel. His horrible vision of the Antichrist might have staggered him physically and psychologically, but his sickness only lasted a matter of days. There was no room in his makeup for any sort of cynicism. His heart remained filled with a strong hope. After earnest prayer and fasting, he got up again and carried on King Belshazzar's business with greater dedication.

I wish I could say the same for Daniel Carr. My sickness lasted many months, not just a few days, and there were times when I was filled with depression and unhappiness. Over and over again I would ask, "Why me, Lord?" It was a long time before I received the answer to that question. But, at long last, I could finally say with Job of old, "He knows the way I take; and when He has tried me, I shall come forth as gold" (Job 23:10). What a thrill it was to realize that God had put me through this long refining process in order to ready me for a new way that I should take. This way led me to actual work among the Nosu tribespeople as well as the Chinese.

Our mission society in the States had previously decided that one of our main instruments in reaching the Nosu to the north would be a medical ministry and had even appointed a doctor whose desire was to serve there.

We had consulted and prayed with Dr. James Broomhall of the China Inland Mission. He was a medical missionary from England who arrived in Xichang with his family and co-workers shortly before us and was planning a medical ministry in the southern part of Nosuland. He was very much in favor of our starting a medical work to the north in the town of Lugu which was about thirty miles from Xichang and right on the border of Independent Nosuland.

The mission felt led of the Lord to occupy Lugu. Ralph Covell and Yang Jiehmin (our national evangelist) and his wife moved to this town on February 3, 1949, rented a street chapel with living quarters connected to it, and opened up our work there. Land had already been purchased and it was to be the site of a hospital. Ralph was to supervise the construction of the first building on this property. The plan called for the Carrs to live in it until the arrival of medical personnel.

The mission had decided that Lucille would wait in Xichang until my return from Shanghai, and then we were to move to Lugu. However, since my return seemed so indefinite and a missionary lady was urgently needed in Lugu, it was thought best that she should go on ahead with the children and our amah just as soon as the hospital building was finished.

Ralph went to Xichang to escort them to Lugu. There was a big question as to whether or not they should make the move at this time since travel between the two towns was very dangerous due to periodic fighting between the local tribes. Despite the situation, it was decided that they should make the trip. The trip, made by ricksha and bicycle, was arduous with many waist deep river crossings. When they finally reached Lugu late at night, they were challenged by soldiers who stood guard and things were tense until they were able to satisfactorily identify themselves.

What a relief it was when the tribal warfare was settled shortly after their arrival. About 3,000 Nationalist soldiers had been sent in to occupy the town. The number of soldiers just about equalled the local population itself. Many feasts were held to celebrate the conclusion of the fighting and the missionaries were invited to attend.

Lucille was particularly happy, for it meant that she could leave the confines of her walled quarters on a hill outside the town and travel freely through the town and neighboring villages. In a letter written in August 1949, she had this to say about our new adobe home overlooking Lugu:

We're delighted with our new home. The house itself might not look like a mansion on Nob Hill, but it's comfortable. The walls are made of mud and straw mixed together, tamped, allowed to dry, and then whitewashed. The roof is covered with tile. Toilet facilities are on the outside. The building is divided into five sections and surrounded by a customary six-foot wall topped with glass shards to keep out unwanted guests. The windows are covered with oiled paper to keep the rain out. Kerosene lamps provide light and our water is carried from a river about a quarter of a mile away.

The scenery is gorgeous! I wish you could stand with us on our little hill and look down on the cluster of houses that make up Lugu, and look beyond as the river winds its silvery way through the green valley, and then look up as mountains with their majestic peaks and lofty ridges jut into the heavens.

Just a few miles to the west you can see a little village. You can even spot the tall tree in which the Bible woman and I found some children playing the other day. They gladly climbed down to look at pictures and hear us tell a Bible story. They listened eagerly and invited us back. When we returned the following week, we found a courtyard swept clean and benches prepared. Soon there were about eighty people gathered around us listening attentively to the story of the Prodigal Son. They also heard us sing a song about our Heavenly Father, the one true God, who feeds, clothes, and cares for us. They responded to our speaking and singing by saying, "What you say is true. Who doesn't believe in God?" But they believe in many gods, and what we said about Christ scarcely registered with them. Please pray that as we go each week to this village there might be many who will say they not only believe in a god but that they believe in the One True God and in his Son, Jesus Christ.

Our hill serves as a grazing ground for horses, goats, Tibetan yak, and water buffalo which give it added interest to the children. It's fun to watch the little buffalo herders riding on the broad backs of the stolid buffalo. One of the boys had an especially pleasant smile; so after talking with him for awhile, I asked if he'd like to hear a story. Other children came, too, and a rock pile in front of our house made a good speaker's platform. We've promised a story hour once a week for them, for they have no free time to come to our street chapel. Remember to pray that they might learn to love the One who is the Good Shepherd.

Last night from our hill you would have seen a very colorful sight—fires at the doorway of almost every home. The people were doing far more than just paying their respects to their ancestors. They were actually worshipping them. They had spent several days preparing paper money and other paper objects and then burning them, trusting they would materialize in the Buddhist hell for their ancestors' use.

It hurt us to see even tiny children bowing around the big pile of ashes. I'm sure Satan gets quite a kick out of it though and looks at us as if to say, "See, this is my territory and I'm keeping it." It certainly is in his clutches right now—fear, superstition, opium, death. This is his domain. You can see a narrow path to the east. Up that path, a two-day journey, is Yuexi. There is no witness between here and there—none there. But there aren't enough of us to carry the Gospel to

> *Yuexi now. To the north is a much broader road leading to Mianning. All along that road are small villages in darkness; and at the end of a day's journey, the traveler will find that Mianning has never heard the message of Redeeming Love. If he makes the two-day journey south to Xichang, he will find no Christian witness along the way. To the west is a broad expanse of Chinese and Tibetan villages unreached by the Gospel, an area with which we are scarcely acquainted. In the surrounding mountains are countless Nosu tribespeople who have never heard the story of Jesus and his love. How we hate to even consider the possibility of having to leave this very needy area because of a Communist takeover.*

Having experienced the Communist takeover of Shanghai, I was able to share my wife's concern about a Communist victory on our field when I finally returned to her and the children in December of 1949. Such a victory seemed quite imminent and we were very anxious to reach as many people as possible in the area before being forced out of China.

Following the same pattern that we had used in Xichang, we started our new work in Lugu by witnessing first of all to our Chinese constituency on the streets of the town and in the surrounding villages. One day, to use the Chinese expression, we walked about "forty minutes' worth" of country roads to a village that we weren't able to get to regularly. When we arrived, one person said, "It's no use to come today. Come back some other time. Most of the people are out gathering opium in the poppy fields." But just as soon as I started playing my accordion, a big crowd appeared on the scene and listened attentively as I sang and told them of Jesus.

The last days of February saw the finish of the Chinese New Year's festivities and I took stock of the whole affair with a feeble attempt at verse:

> *With rooting and tooting and dragons a-roaring*
> *And gambling and scrambling mixed up in the stew,*
> *We found ourselves lamely and vainly imploring*
> *Deliverance from this wild hullabaloo.*

> *Then something constrained us until it did pain us*
> *For out of the din of this New Year's stew*
> *A Voice did behoove us and surely did move us*
> *To seek for Himself His aforechosen few.*

And so we did both in Lugu and Mianning. Lucille and our Bible women spent a busy nine days in Lugu conducting daily services for women and children and trying to ward off literally hundreds of Chinese and Nosu who made a New Year's trek to the home of these strange "foreign devils." Ralph and I, along with our Chinese evangelist, Yang Jiemin, and our cook's son, left the wild hullabaloo and walked twenty-five miles north to Mianning, the county seat, where we preached the Gospel for nine days.

We left Lugu at 8:30 on the morning of the eighteenth and arrived in Mianning at 5:30 that night—nine hours to walk twenty-five miles. I'm sure my youngest child, Jim, could have crawled that far in the same amount of time. But out there in those parts, we had to stick with our opium-smoking carriers who walk a minute and rest five. Letting them out of our sight might have meant saying goodbye to our belongings, and I wasn't too anxious to let my accordion provide the bellows for some Chinese forge.

Our lodging place in Mianning turned out to be a gambling den operated by the chief of police, and thus we found ourselves lulled to sleep each night by the rattling of "mah-jongg" chips. Several nights they rattled the whole night through. Our complaints of not being able to sleep because of their infernal noise were met by their complaints of not being able to concentrate because of our infernal snoring. Now Ralph and I will swear to the fact that we just do not snore—nothing more than a little heavy breathing.

Each day found us out on the streets and in our meeting hall seeking those whom He had chosen. It was quite a job, considering the fact that practically all of these folk were hearing the Gospel for the first time. That plus the fact that these people were steeped in sin and superstition made the job a difficult one. We learned from a Chinese Catholic priest that only fifteen or so had embraced Roman Catholicism in approximately fifteen years. The record was even worse in our own town of Lugu—seven converts to the Catholic Church in fifteen years.

"THEN I GOT UP AGAIN ..."

Mianning was a walled city with a population of some 10,000 and was, along with Xichang and Huili, one of the three important towns in the valley. The town was so laid out that it made for an excellent routine of daily witnessing. Four main streets running north, south, east, and west merged at a large tower in the center of the town to form a perfect cross. Our daily plan called for a rotation of outside meetings on each of these four streets. One day it would be North Street in the morning and South Street in the afternoon— the next day, East Street in the morning and West Street in the afternoon.

Our usual procedure was for me to start playing the accordion at the central tower and then we would march together up one branch of the cross until a sizeable crowd had gathered. Then a service would be held lasting from an hour and a half to two hours. A daily service was held for children at 5:00 P.M. in a meeting hall located near the center of town followed by a general evangelistic service at 6:30—four services a day with all of us sounding forth daily. The crowds in general were quite attentive and listened well. Of course the usual few rowdies were always present with their wisecracks and occasional stones.

In addition to the spoken word, Gospel tracts were pasted on the more important walls of the town and several thousand Gospel excerpts and tracts were distributed at all meetings. Yes, the town of Mianning really got "the once and many times over" with the

Gospel. Our visit became the subject of a poem written by a local sage describing our style of witnessing, including the plastering of walls with Christian literature.

One of our days was spent preaching at the gate of a temple located on a mountain south of town. This day was an important one in the Buddhist calendar and brought many of the townsfolk to the temple to pay homage to the gods. There we caught them with the Word coming and going.

After nine intense and exciting days of preaching the Word in Mianning, we returned to Lugu and made plans to include Mianning in our regular program of work. The seed that was sown there and in the other towns had to be watered even though we were afraid that we just didn't have enough workers and time to cover such a widespread ministry.

The women were carrying out an equally intense effort in Lugu and the closer villages. Lucille and the Bible woman moved up one street and down the next inviting women to the weekly meetings in our street chapel. Since the women in town didn't have the slightest

"THEN I GOT UP AGAIN ..."

idea what day of the week it was, they had to be invited on the very day of the meeting or the attendance would be nil. I'll let Lucille take you on one of her visitation rounds:

> *First, let us stop at this little house over to the left. We'd better not go in for there's certain to be someone lying on the bed smoking opium. It is the family's main source of income as well as its greatest sorrow, for the mother is held in its grasp, as are most of the other people in our town. "We'd like you to come to the meeting tonight and hear more about Christ," we tell her. "But I've nothing to wear (an excuse used by women around the world). We're so wretched. If only you could give me some medicine to help me overcome this habit." We tell her again of the One who can help, but it scarcely penetrates.*
>
> *On up a pretty little lane, we call again on an old Muslim lady whose roof had caved in and because of poverty is forced to live in the open, but that doesn't seem to daunt her. We try to show her how Allah has not helped her and how Christ can meet her need, but she keeps replying, "I'll believe in Allah until I die." We pass a whole street of Muslim people who seem to share her empty faith, but some of them promise to come to the chapel to hear more about this man Jesus.*
>
> *Now we'll make our way to a very modest home where an old lady sits bent over her loom. She's been busily making grass sandals all morning and her face lights up as we approach. "I was just thinking of you," she says, "and am glad you have come. So many things you tell me I can't remember, but I keep thinking of God and trying to pray to Him." We sit on little stools and talk as she weaves her grass thread. Again we explain the things we had explained before and are amazed at how quickly she grasps the Gospel message.*
>
> *We are so accustomed to explaining the Word over and over again without the listener having the vaguest idea what it's all about that we feel certain that the Holy Spirit has been working in the heart of this 70-year-old woman who so clearly*

understands the way of salvation and who so sincerely says she believes. Now she lays aside the sandals for a few minutes, closes her trachoma-dimmed eyes and asks the Father to forgive and take her as His child. Then she returns to her work, but her back seems straighter and her eyes brighter. How our hearts rejoice as we leave her.

On down the street we go inviting all the women within sight. We'll stop on the bridge a moment to talk with several women who are selling peanuts, dried peppers, and cotton thread. Two of them are Buddhist vegetarians but are willing to listen as we tell them that works such as keeping a vegetarian vow cannot save them—only Christ. But it's routine from here on out with many of the women promising to come but never coming and others pointedly saying that they will not come.

Well, we've finished our rounds, but please remember these women in your prayers. Remember especially that one dear old lady at work making sandals. She needs prayer now, for we've seen Satan at work around here before. Just as soon as some are on the verge of believing he does his vile work and causes them to lose all interest. This woman needs prayer for another reason, too. We didn't have a chance to tell you her story while we were visiting with her. We learned from her daughter the reason for her diligence at work, for the poverty in her home, for the scarcity of food when we've happened in at meal times and for the raggedness of apparel.

The daughter who lives with her has been married some fifteen years and has had four sons, but only two are at home. Where are the other two? One twelve and the other fifteen were sold into Nosu slavery by her worthless husband who wanted the money to support his opium habit. One she cannot contact, but the other has been gone only two years and is in the mountains about ten miles north of here. The mother knows where he is and can buy him back for three lumps of silver—a mere fifteen dollars in U.S. currency but a fortune to them. They had worked and saved nearly the required amount when the husband made one of his rare *appearances, stayed a few days, and went away with everything they had saved.*

The family was very grateful when we covered the ransom amount. We rejoiced with them over the son's ransom from Nosu slavery, but we would have rejoiced even more if they had accepted the ransom paid by our Savior, Jesus Christ, on the Cross of Calvary. The daughter and her sons showed very little interest in the Savior; but the dear, old grandmother, Mrs. Jou, continued to show a real interest and soon allowed Christ to enter her heart. She was our first convert in Lugu and very faithful in her attendance at our chapel services.

It always amazed me how Lucille could do such a fine job of taking care of her husband and children and still find the time and energy to be an integral part of the general missionary program of the station. While making our home a haven of rest for her family and lighthouse to all who were attracted to it, she still found time each day to go out in the highways and byways and tell others about Christ.

Lucille was also aware of the frailties of womanhood and often told how Eve had passed the buck with the words, "The serpent beguiled me." Though she has always loathed snakes, she still didn't like them being blamed for something of which they are not guilty. But they were blamed in the story that she heard one day. Our son Danny told her how our dog had seen two snakes and jumped all over the place in his excitement.

"Where?" she asked. "Among the graves in the cemetery next to our compound," was his reply. Danny was just at that age where the line between truth and fiction grows very thin, so she passed it off as another product of his very fertile imagination. The little rascal, perceiving that she didn't believe him, was incensed and called the cook to verify his story. "Yes, it's true," he said; but he wasn't satisfied with just substantiating Danny's story. He had to add another layer to it. "Male and female snakes are rarely seen together," he continued, "and we believe that death comes to all who look upon them."

She laughed and asked, "Who saw them?" "Lin San Jieh (the Lin family's third daughter), her mother, Danny and Jimmy, and my wife," he replied. "Lin San Jieh has since died and my wife is seriously ill." Actually, his wife had nothing more than a common illness which soon disappeared. She wanted to tell the cook that San Jieh's death was the work of another serpent—a very subtle and deadly one—but knew he wouldn't understand. This girl had been a vegetarian and had spent a number of years as a Buddhist nun in a local temple. She became interested in the Gospel shortly after our arrival and often came to our home to study the Word. Then one night in our living room, she fell on her knees and begged forgiveness. However when we offered her cookies containing pork lard with the hope that she would eat them and break her vegetarian vow, thus proving that her repentance was real, she refused and went her way. She had vowed not to eat any meat or meat products such as pork lard.

For several months she avoided us. Then one day she met my wife in a neighboring cornfield and said she wanted to give up her vegetarian vow and believe in the Lord. Lucille talked with her for a long time but felt that her motive was not right. Her body was covered with sores and she wanted God to heal them. The two of them spent many hours together in that little thatched shelter out in the field where she watched the corn. Since thieves and beggars were plentiful in the area, all who would harvest a crop had to live next to it day and night.

After many sessions in the Word, San Jieh affirmed her faith in Christ and proved it by eating cookies made with lard and by witnessing boldly to her family and relatives who all lived together on the same compound. They watched her break her vegetarian vow by eating meat in front of them.

Unfortunately, San Jieh didn't respond to the skin treatment that we gave her, so we ordered a special drug from Xichang. When it arrived, Lucille went to her home and asked for her. She was stunned when her mother unexpectedly replied, "She's been murdered!" After recovering from the shock, Lucille pieced the story together. The young son and wife of her landlord had clubbed her to death, angered at her breaking the vegetarian vow. Our cook attributed all this to the snake encounter, but we knew it was that old serpent, the Devil.

It wasn't enough to be bothered by serpents. We were also bothered by dragons—dragon kings who were directly under the command of the great Heavenly Emperor. It all started when we experienced a terrible drought in our area. Now there are many ways of "producing" rain in China. Let me describe two of them. One day, while returning home from a workers' prayer meeting (not especially for rain), we came upon a dozen or more scantily clad men with willow branches draped around their bodies and over their heads. They danced madly up one street and down another stopping long enough at each house for a bucket of water to be poured over their heads, firmly believing that these strange antics would win the pleasure of the heavenly emperor and cause him to grant rain. Apparently their efforts were of no avail for soon afterwards we heard that the gods were going to be sunned, so off we went to see just how potent this new method would prove in "stirring" their fickle heavenly royalty. The gods are sunned after all other rain-producing methods fail. This was to be the big test.

It is a common belief among the people that dragon kings control the rainfall under the direction of the Heavenly Emperor. Therefore, during times of drought, images of these gods are hauled out of their temples and paraded through the streets under the scorching rays of the sun. In this way the images are made to taste the sufferings of the people in the drought area, thus causing them to produce rain for their own relief as well as for their worshippers. "Now that you've shared our suffering," the people pray, "do give us rain. If you'll only give us rain, we'll carry you back to the temple and worship you more fervently than we've ever done before."

While praying for rain, the last thing in the world these people want is for the rain to be accompanied by a hail storm. Such a storm destroys their crops. When hail storms do occur, they are accompanied by a noisy volley of shots which echo throughout the entire valley and almost shatter our ear drums. As soon as the hail hits the ground, the farmers grab their guns and fire madly into the sky to scare off the devils plaguing the valley with hail. Since these storms usually last only a few minutes, the people are absolutely convinced that their firing of guns was successful in scaring the devils away.

What these Chinese people in the valley really needed was a hail storm lasting for several hours—one that would have caused them to run out of ammunition, curse the gods for letting them down, and heed the message that we gave them over and over again that Jesus Christ is the Way, the Truth, and the Life. This was the same wonderful message that we wanted to give to the Nosu "on the mountains."

"THEN I GOT UP AGAIN ..."

Chapter 17

"ON THE MOUNTAINS"

"How lovely on the mountains are the feet of him who brings good news, who announces peace and brings good news of happiness, who announces salvation ..." (Isaiah 52:7)

Even though the reference in Isaiah 52 has to do with the heralds who went on in advance of the returning Babylonian exiles to announce to the inhabitants of Jerusalem that they would see the Lord restore Zion, it also implies the beauty of all those messengers who proclaim the good news of salvation. It even included those of us who were anxious to tell the same good news to all the people living in the valleys and mountains of Nosuland.

It was not enough for us just to proclaim the good news to the Chinese living in our valley. We also needed to proclaim it to the Nosu tribespeople who lived on the mountains surrounding our valley, but how were we to reach them? It would have been absolutely foolhardy for us to just start walking up the trails to their mountain villages. Those trails were guarded by rugged tribesmen who would kill any stranger daring to use them. Furthermore, these mountain tribes were always fighting among themselves. Each tribe claimed it's own portion of the mountains. Woe be to the tribe on one mountain that trespassed on the mountain of another tribe. The Nosu were never to be seen without their rifles. I remember the time soon after our arrival in Xichang that Lucille and I joined the Jim Garrisons in a little walk up a trail to a mountain village just outside the town. We had only gone about a quarter of a mile when rifle bullets whizzed by our heads. We wasted no time in dashing back to the gates of the town.

The tribespeople would often come into our towns for supplies. Those who lived in mountains close to Chinese towns could speak Chinese. Those who lived back deeper in the mountains could only speak their own native tongue. Ralph Covell had a special call to translate the Bible into the tribal tongue and found Nosu informants to help him with the language.

"ME? A MISSIONARY?"

Some of the Nosu who could understand Chinese would wander into the meetings in our little street chapel. I remember the time I was teaching the people to sing a little chorus. The words were taken from Luke 5:32, "I came not to call the righteous, but sinners to repentance." Every time we sang that chorus the Nosu would sit there with smug smiles on their faces. Puzzled, I asked our Chinese evangelist if he knew the reason for their smiles. Oh yes, he knew. It all revolved around the use of one little tone. I have already mentioned the tonal quality of the Chinese language.

In the natural singing of the song, the Chinese word for "righteous" (pronounced "yee"), a first tone word, drops naturally into a second tone which changes the meaning to the Chinese word for "Nosu" (also pronounced "yee"). So, instead of singing, "I came not to call the righteous, but sinners to repentance," we were singing, "I came not to call the Nosu (they are the righteous ones), but sinners (the Chinese) to repentance." This all resulted in our having to substitute the word "good" for "righteous."

One might be able to appreciate the satisfied Nosu smiles when singing this song if reminded of the hatred between the Nosu and the Chinese. These tribal people, the original inhabitants of our area, were driven up into the rugged mountains by the Chinese who came in and occupied all the fertile valleys. As with any conquered people driven from their land, the Nosu hatred of the Chinese was deep and often found expression in the capture of Chinese to be held as slaves.

Our relationship with the Chinese and Nosu on our field required some difficult and not always successful fence straddling. We were frowned upon by the Chinese for being friendly with the Nosu and frowned upon by the Nosu for being friendly with the Chinese. Though the Chinese frowned upon our dealing with the Nosu, we went ahead with our plan to reach the Nosu through a medical ministry. That's why we erected our first hospital building on a hill OUTSIDE the walls of Lugu.

While living in that "hospital" building waiting for qualified medical personnel to arrive and begin the medical ministry, it occurred to me that I could go ahead and open a little dispensary inside the town. When I suggested this to Ralph and Lucille they asked, "What do you know about medicine?" My simple response was, "What do these people know about medicine? They look only to their many gods and goddesses for healing."

I could trust in the One True God for help and I had in my possession a full trunk of medical supplies which included the new "wonder drugs" (penicillin and sulfa), sutures, bandages, etc. These supplies had been given to me by Navy doctors when I was still a Navy chaplain and a patient in the Philadelphia Naval Hospital at the end of the war. They wanted to make a contribution to my proposed missionary work in China. They also gave me about a dozen medical textbooks. The only other medical preparation that I had was first-aid training as a chaplain that would enable me to work with medical corpsmen under battle conditions.

At last, with the help of our evangelist's wife, Mrs. Yang, who had taken a few courses in nursing, we opened a simple clinic in our chapel on the main street of town. We also prayed that Ralph might marry Ruth Laube, a new missionary arrival in Xichang. Afterall, there did appear to be a noticeable spark between them. Ralph certainly seemed to lose some of his composure whenever he was around her. I was also quick to notice that Ruth was a registered nurse as well as a very fine person.

In the meantime, I began treating bullet wounds, opium addiction, dermatitis, trachoma, simple colds, stomach ailments, diarrhea, tape worms, roundworms, dysentery, malaria, venereal and other kinds of diseases, trusting that my patients would not die from my ministrations. Relatives of the deceased might put an end to the work of a "quack" doctor permanently and were known to have attacked even trained medical personnel in Chinese hospitals. God was faithful and merciful in watching over our attempts to meet the physical needs of the people. Before opening the clinic for treatment, we conducted a short service in which we explained the Gospel message. Lucille then sat at the main entrance of the clinic, interviewing and screening all the patients before turning them over to me. Some of the cases were so grotesque that I became ill and on more than one occasion I actually ran out of the clinic and vomited. For instance, there was an unkempt Nosu who came to us with a festering bullet wound that he had plastered with manure. Reflecting later (after losing my lunch), I concluded that the man had probably done the right thing afterall. It could be that the warm manure poultice had actually helped to draw the pus out of the wound.

We could only open our clinic two afternoons a week since we needed time for outstation work, time to cover a dozen or more towns and villages. What we really needed was a score of additional workers. Why even one or two more would have helped out tremendously. We could only see about fifty patients in our clinic each day, even though many more people were anxious to be seen. Many were finding real relief because of our efforts and a steady stream of sick folk came to us as the news of our medical "magic" was noised around the town and even in the mountains.

The Nosu, who were not too keen on mingling with the Chinese, rarely came to our clinic in town. They did, however, come to our home on the hill and ask for help. Unfortunately, many of them came too late and died outside our gate. One of our biggest problems was trying to enforce our sanitary rules. The Nosu, like the Tibetans, were not in the habit of bathing themselves and made no effort to keep themselves clean. They would not follow our directions and tore off their bandages soon after leaving our compound. The soap that we gave them was never used. Another problem was trying to get the patient to take his medication at given times rather than consume it all at one time. This meant that we would often have them come to us each day for medication. Despite these problems, we still treated all those who came to us for help.

How surprised we were one day when Lo Ziqin, the most powerful Nosu chieftain in our area, entered our compound with three of his five wives (rather unusual among the Nosu) and children, and a whole retinue of armed attendants. They wandered through our house and then squatted on the ground outside with their long black capes draped around them, listening to Chinese hymns being played on our little phonograph and smiling at Danny who sat there with them. They are mountaineers and love music. They kept looking for the people who were producing the music in that little box.

I took the chief aside and worked on his skin infection. Later one of the babies squalled as it felt the strange sensation of a good scrubbing followed by the application of sulfa ointment and bandaging for its scabbies. Another baby needed medicine for its red, bleary eyes infected with trachoma, and one of the hardened mountain warriors winced as I soaked his badly crushed hand in a hot solution.

The result of all this was our cook preparing a chicken dinner for us. The Nosu had given us that chicken in appreciation of our services. The day before, some Chinese patients of ours had brought some fish and eggs in appreciation. It all tasted good to us for we noticed that this ministry was leaving a good taste in the mouths of our patients, too, and that was very important if we were to reach them with the Gospel.

A few days later, two armed Nosu came to escort us to the mountain retreat of the Nosu chief mentioned above. We kept up a pretty fast pace going up a mountain trail, and let me emphasize the word "up." When it comes to travel, the Nosu always travel the shortest distance between two points. In this case, it was "up."

We had been to Nosu villages before but not as invited guests. They were all out to meet us. We didn't spot them at first for they were too well-blended into the rocky hillside above us. The chief graciously ushered us into his fortress with its gun tower rising about three stories above the walls. We sat on the ground in true Nosu fashion, wondering what was coming next. Then we heard it! The squeals of a doomed pig filled the courtyard. Out came the knife, the blood squirted freely, and we understood a bit more about the Biblical custom of killing a fatted calf—only this was the fatted pig which had to be killed in front of the honored guests to assure them that the meat was fresh and that it was prepared especially for them.

We were then led to a circular spot where a roaring fire was ready in their hole-in-the-ground fireplace to sear the pig thoroughly. One man had a hoe, another just a crude stick, but both proved effective in removing the hair from the pig. Then it was cut up and a number of pieces thrown into the fire.

Not more than an hour after the pig had made its appearance, we were sitting on the ground around the fire eating the most delicious roast pork we'd ever tasted. It was placed on a very low table and we helped ourselves—with our fingers, of course. With a piece of pork in one hand and a roasted potato in the other, we ate our fill, not realizing there would be more to come. Then appeared a large bowl of rice and more meat plus the very tasty soup that can only be made from a newly slaughtered pig. Plates and chopsticks were not to be had, but rather a very cleverly designed wooden spoon with a long handle served as both dish and eating utensil.

While the menfolk talked, one of the wives of the chief showed my wife around the compound. At one house, they gave her some "zanba" which is just oatmeal mixed with water—a favorite with their cousins, the Tibetans. The chief's wife used her unwashed hands to mould it into a ball for Lucille and, as she sat on the ground eating it, the women sat around her, smoking their pipes. Incidentally, they used a glass lens to ignite their pipe tobacco.

Our visit ended with the chief presenting us with the pig's head—the Nosu way of honoring guests. As we walked the six miles home, we met many Nosu returning to the area from which we had just come. They all looked knowingly at the pig's head and asked where we had eaten, for they knew we had been in one of their homes. All of them seemed quite pleased and we, of course, were pleased, for this meant that we were another step closer to reaching these people from a land described by our friend, Dr. James Broomhall, as "a mountain territory of wild tribesmen which strangers enter at their peril." In his book, *Strong Man's Prey* (London: China Inland Mission, 1953), Broomhall tells about his work in the southern part of Nosuland. He characterizes the Nosu as follows:

> *The ravages of wine and opium addiction had been plain enough since the first contacts with them in Juheh and Zhaojue. Feuds, injuries, gambling debts, disease, depravity, theft, and robbery all stemmed from them. In every stage, from playful cup or whiff to grand debauchery, the abuse was apparent ...*
>
> *Opium smoking was a widespread habit among the Nosu, but by no means as extensive as wine drinking. A sure way of pleasing them was to treat them to a drink. The Chinese officials seldom called a parley without pouring out a basin-full, from which the Nosu dipped with rice bowls and drank until they could say contentedly, with a flushed face and slurred speech, "Goodbye, I'm nicely drunk now."*

Broomhall also mentions how Captain Scott, the Antarctic explorer, wrote about how on his last expedition his companions entertained each other in the long, winter hours with tales of their adventures. "One of the most fascinating stories had been about Nosuland, a feast in a 'barbaric hall hung with skins and weapons, the men clad in buckskin dyed red and bristling with arms,' and a tragedy in which the speaker's friend, Lieutenant Francis Brooke, had been killed by the Nosu." These events actually took place about thirty miles to the east of our town of Lugu in an area occupied by the fierce Nosu Ahu clan—the clan that killed Brooke. Broomhall also has much to say about the barbarous Nosu practice of capturing people and making them slaves.

Well, so far in our work among the Nosu we had not yet become their slaves nor had we lost our heads. The Nosu not only took people as slaves, they took heads. I vividly remember the shock I received one day in Xichang while standing in front of the police station. Some policemen arrived with a Nosu man who was carrying a large sack. He was told to dump the contents of the sack on the ground. This he did and several human heads, still bleeding, rolled out onto the ground. One of them hit my leg. This tribesman and several others had taken these heads while raiding a mountain village.

Praise the Lord! Instead of taking our heads, the Nosu had taken us into their hearts. They had accepted us as their friends. The chief who had invited us to his mountain stronghold promised to station a Nosu guard around our residence and chapel in case of trouble and, if things got too dangerous, he'd take us to the safety of his mountain stronghold.

Even though many of the Nosu had become our friends, others remained our enemies and would have gladly done away with us. The Chinese living within the relative safety of Lugu thought we were crazy to live outside of town altogether unprotected from Nosu attack. Our cook's wife wasn't impressed by the protection offered us by the friendly Nosu and assumed she was doing us a big favor by passing around the word that we had a formidable arsenal in our home and that all of us, including the women, were crack shots. She also announced that fierce watchdogs guarded our property. The well-intentioned woman didn't realize that she was actually inviting a Nosu raid on our home, for the Nosu would kill in order to secure firearms.

Yes, we made many friends among the people on our field of work, but Satan made sure that we also had our enemies. Despite this fact, I continued to praise God for allowing me to continue witnessing even "in the presence of my enemies."

"ON THE MOUNTAINS"

"ME? A MISSIONARY?"

Chapter 18

"IN THE PRESENCE OF MY ENEMIES"

"Thou dost prepare a table before me in the presence of my enemies ..." (Psalm 23:5)

The Psalmist David was an expert in using pastoral imagery. When he wrote this psalm, he was probably looking back to his days as a shepherd. As he had watched over his flock and protected them from beasts of prey, he must have felt confident that his God would provide for him and protect him from all his enemies. This is how we felt as the Communists began to slowly make their way toward our area. The situation was such that our missionaries in Xichang sent word to all of our stations that they had received the following message from American Consular officials:

Communist thrusts to the south and west make it essential to consider leaving China while the way is still open. Certainly women and children should do so. There is no knowing how the situation may deteriorate. No responsibility can be shouldered by the government for those who fail to follow this advice while it is possible to travel.

After receiving this word from the Embassy and much prayer, our missionaries felt led of the Lord to remain at their posts with their families.

In March of 1950 I was startled by a loud pounding on our compound gate. I rushed to the gate and threw it open and found myself staring into the faces of four men in uniform with red stars on their caps. I shouted, "Who are you?" They shouted back, "Your liberators!"

Well, to tell the truth, though I really wasn't too much interested in their liberating me, I felt it wise to invite them into our compound. This they refused. For some reason or another, they were afraid to enter and kept ordering me, "Come out! Come out!" while I kept repeating, "Come in! Come in!" Observing that their trigger fingers were beginning to tremble just a little too much, I finally thought it was the better part of valor to obey their order.

When I roughly threw open the gate, one of the soldiers was actually so frightened he fell over backwards on the ground. I found out later that some of the people in town had told them that we were harboring some Nationalist troops on our compound. Undoubtedly they thought I was about to lead a Nationalist charge when the gate flew open.

This was our "liberation" by the troops of the People's Republic of China. That night a heavily-armed squad of soldiers entered our compound, pitched their tents, and posted a guard. As evening approached, they suddenly decided to pack up their gear and head for the safety of our walled town. When I questioned the officer in charge, he simply pointed his finger toward the Nosu villages on the hills above us and said, "You people are leaving yourselves wide open to an attack by those tribespeople. We have fought all over China, including Tibet, but we've never faced a fiercer group of people than the Nosu." He then suggested that we, too, should move into town. Xichang, our mission headquarters and the last Nationalist stronghold in Mainland China, had fallen a few days earlier to three columns of Red soldiers advancing from the south. Shortly before their arrival, General He, the commanding Nationalist general, and a number of his high-ranking officers escaped by plane to Formosa (Taiwan), leaving behind their leaderless soldiers to face the oncoming Communist army. Many of these soldiers shed their military uniforms and fled to the mountains, hoping to stay there until the start of World War III. They had believed rumors that America would come to their aid. One rumor was that thousands of American paratroopers had landed to the south and were on their way north. All of these rumors proved false. Much to their sorrow, these troops found themselves set upon by the tribal people. Just a few days before the takeover of our town, many Chinese Nationalist soldiers and Chinese civilians were robbed and left absolutely naked by the Nosu in a village just twenty miles to the east of us. One report claimed that 2,000 of them had been killed, but the figure was probably too high. Many of these poor refugees poured into Lugu and Mrs. Yang and I did our best to treat those who had been stoned, beaten and shot by the Nosu. We were also able to give the naked ones some "white cross" relief clothing.

"IN THE PRESENCE OF MY ENEMIES"

The arrival of Communist troops at this particular time probably prevented a much greater slaughter. Though the Communists weren't pleased with our helping "the enemy," they didn't give us any trouble as we treated these Nationalist soldiers and civilians. Actually, the Communists had troubles of their own. Their troops coming up from the south arrived in our vicinity about the same time as their troops coming down from the north. A battle took place with many casualties before these two armies realized they were all on the same side. This was the last place to be liberated in China. Fortunately, we were also able to help some of these wounded Red soldiers as they came to our clinic for help.

With the help of Mrs. Yang, I began digging bullets out of the bodies of these soldiers, sewing them up, dispensing medicines, and wondering why they hadn't gone to their own medical corpsmen. When I asked them about this, they told me that their own medical people didn't know anything about medicine. I'm afraid I had to agree with them.

About this time, a couple came to our home and asked me to save their thirty-year-old daughter who had just taken an overdose of opium in a suicide attempt. Suicides were very common in our area. I rushed to the home, found the woman in a coma, shoved my finger down her throat, caused her to vomit, and saw her on the road to recovery. When I left the home to help in a street meeting, I warned the parents not to let anybody give her medicine before my return that night. Returning after the meeting, I found that the daughter had died. A Communist medical team, trying to win favor in the town, went into the home and gave her a massive overdose of adrenalin, a heart stimulant. Empty glass vials were all over the dirt floor. This medicine had come from tons of American drugs turned over to them by surrendering Nationalist armies.

The new responsibility of treating the military as well as civilians caused me quite a bit of concern. I began to question my ability to carry this load. What if I should make a mistake? Certainly the Lord must have known that I was heading for a big fall as far as my medical "expertise" was concerned, so he answered my prayer for a qualified medical person by seeing to it that Ralph Covell and Ruth Laube were united in marriage by Bill Simons at a service in Xichang on May 26, 1950. It was my happy privilege to stand as Ralph's best man. This meant that Lugu would have a qualified nurse, and Mrs. Yang and I would be her assistants. How glad I was to turn the medical responsibilities over to Ruth. No longer would I have to tremble over the possibility of making the wrong diagnosis.

I happily supervised the conversion of our home into a two-family facility. Mrs. Jiang, our amah and Bible woman, had already left us and returned to her home province of Shandong. We occupied three sections of the building and the Covells occupied the other two. Since more space was needed, the attic was converted into a second story. This worked well just so long as the person walked erect in the middle of it and ducked on the sides which were no more that four feet high. I don't know how many times I bumped my head before getting used to this new arrangement, but I didn't care how many times I bumped my head if it meant having a registered nurse on the team.

One day Lo Bimo, a Nosu sorcerer-priest, rushed to our compound and asked medical aid for his wife—a very unusual thing for a bimo in good standing to do. Perhaps he came in a moment of weakness; but the fact still remains, HE CAME! Dr. Broomhall says this about these bimos:

> *These sorcerer priests are the only ones able to read the racial writings, ancient manuscripts containing tribal history and incantations for use on all religious occasions. The knowledge was passed on with the office, from father to son, and the devilry of ancient times was thus perpetuated. All the benightedness of the race was concentrated in these men, amiable farmers when not performing their specific functions. They were wizards, necromancers, exorcists, but above all priests, representatives of the people in offering sacrifices and making contact with the spirits. Up to a hundred years ago human sacrifices had been made in some places, slaves offered up by the noblest lords, but now animal sacrifices are made ... They exhort their listeners about heaven and hell in which they firmly believe, the one a place of joy and the other of torment ... They keep the register of all males born and are in intimate touch with all Nosu homes ... A "bimo" is the supreme spiritual authority over a wide area.*

The Covells and I accompanied Lo Bimo to his home and found that his wife was suffering from a high fever. While we were making preparations to treat her, we noticed the husband cutting three little bamboo sticks about eight inches long and a quarter of an inch in diameter. Oblivious to all that was taking place around him, he silently moved across the room with these three sticks and a rice bowl. After placing a little water in the bottom of the bowl and ordering his wife to dip the fingers of her right hand in it, he waved the bowl over her prostrate body. His next act was to place the bowl on the floor and try to balance the three sticks in the center of it. While this balancing process was going on, he kept calling out the names of devils. We soon awakened to the fact that Lo Bimo was preparing to call a devil out of his wife. Upon our arrival, we had suggested that his wife's fever was probably due to an attack of malaria; but the bimo had insisted that she was demon-possessed.

The naming of devils continued until the name of "Lin Devil" was called out. The sticks immediately stood upright in the bowl. In fact, they seemed to jump right into place. You can imagine the look of surprise that came over our faces and I'm afraid the few

176   "ME? A MISSIONARY?"

remaining hairs on the head of "Yours Truly" stood straight in the air. We looked questioningly at each other and wondered if we had bumped right into the "rulers of the darkness of this world." We were poignantly reminded of the time that Christ called out, "What is your name?" to demons in the maniac of Gadara—the answer being, "My name is 'Legion,' for we are many."

In this case, the alleged name of this particular devil was "Lin." Upon learning the devil's name, the bimo placed some rice in the bowl and mixed it with the three sticks. A little salt was added to give it flavor. He then waved the bowl in circles over his wife and politely called out, "Please, Mr. Lin Devil, come out, come out! Look at this nice tasty bowl of rice. It's yours if you'll only come out!

"IN THE PRESENCE OF MY ENEMIES"

Please! Please come out, Mr. Lin Devil!" Then he moved slowly toward the door and went outside, sprinkling a little of the rice along the way and begging the devil to follow him. When he reached the end of the compound, he flung the remaining portion of rice as far out as he could and then returned to the house.

This was too much for me. I was determined to find out the shenanigans behind this thing. I asked the bimo if he would let us try to stand those sticks on end. He smilingly gave us the "go ahead" signal. Needless to say, we tried and failed. Not satisfied, I asked the bimo if he'd show us how to do it. The whole process was carefully repeated, even to the standing of the sticks when the name "Lin" was called out. But those sticks did not stand for us. When we asked Lo Bimo where he had learned this art, he answered by handing us a little, brown, leather bag filled with scrolls of Nosu script containing incantations for use on all religious occasions and other tribal writings.

I returned home that night with thoughts of this Mr. Lin devil on my mind. The following day I began reading passages in the Bible on demonology and dusting off Augustus H. Strong's *Systematic Theology*. When old "Augustus H." left open some questions regarding the connection of evil spirits with the system of idolatry and witchcraft, I was ready to shout, "Doctor, if you want some real proof, come with me to Nosuland!"

Even today I remain firmly persuaded that "our struggle is not against flesh and blood, but against the rulers, against the powers, against the world forces of this darkness, against the spiritual forces of wickedness in the heavenly places" (Eph. 6:12). I realized then that these spiritual forces of wickedness had a real influence on flesh and blood, especially on the Nosu. Lo Bimo's wife did recover, and I trust that it was the medication that we gave her that brought about this healing.

While focusing a lot of attention on helping the Covells settle down in their new home, I also gave plenty of attention to Lucille as we looked forward to our third child. I was determined that she should have the child in Xichang where Mrs. Madge, a fine British midwife, had taken up residence with her husband. They were missionaries with the Border Service Mission. It took a lot of talking and plenty of pushing, but I was finally able to send Lucille to Xichang to await the arrival of Marilyn Jean. Though she disliked the thought of leaving the boys and me, we felt that she would be in good hands—not the hands of that frightened little Chinese midwife who brought Jimmy into the world. I also felt that the rest in Xichang would do her a world of good. She hadn't had a real vacation since arriving in China and was in need of a big one at this particular time. No one carried a heavier load—mornings filled with housework, clothes making, and the teaching of a home-study Calvert course to young Dan, followed by afternoons of town and country evangelism and visitation and, finally, evening services at our little street chapel. She certainly put me to shame.

I really found out how much Lucille had on her hands after taking over during her absence. On top of it all, I had to bear the brunt of Dan Junior's "Whats" and "Whys." What mosquito protection did they have on Noah's ark? It was only natural that he should ask this question since he always slept under a net to protect himself from mosquitoes and bedbugs. Why did Adam and Eve wear fig leaves? One or two questions would have been alright— even twenty or thirty—but it's another matter when they're thrown at you all day long. Even today he's continually asking questions as an attorney in San Francisco; and according to his wife, Susan, the questioning still goes on daily at their home in San Jose.

I was glad, however, that Danny was becoming a real evangelist. He spoke to our household help daily about their spiritual condition and gave them tracts that he found lying around the house. He did have quite a bit of trouble with the cook's wife. Apparently she was puzzled about the "sin" question—quite a question for a five-year old to tackle. I tried to help him out by answering some of these questions in our morning devotions with our helpers.

During Lucille's absence, Ruth became sick and was bedridden for ten days. This meant that Ralph had to remain on the compound and look after her while I shared in the services at the chapel and covered the medical work. This also meant that Ralph had to watch our two boys during my absences from the compound. I really felt sorry for the poor fellow.

One day I climbed to one of our Nosu villages on top of an 8500 foot mountain and treated a number of tribespeople. It was only a 2500 foot climb since we lived at an altitude of some 6000 feet. Our cook's son went along for the climb and fellowship. He had become quite a zealous Christian and at sixteen years of age he was really interested in the things of the Lord. He loved to witness for the Lord and could always be counted on for a testimony. In fact, I had him lead the singing for me in a service one evening and give a word of testimony. His testimony stretched into a half-hour sermon and caused me to do some fast juggling in order to cut my message short.

When the wonderful news came that Lucille had given birth to Marilyn Jean on September 7, 1950 in Xichang, I immediately set out on my bike for that city to be with Lucille and my first daughter. I left Danny and Jimmy with the Covells. After peddling all day long, I finally arrived in Xichang and was soon holding my wife and daughter in my arms. What a happy time that was and how proud I was the next day to parade my new daughter around the compound for all to see.

The happiness soon changed to bitterness when we tried to return to Lugu. Lucille, Marilyn and I arrived at the main gate of Xichang and were told by the guards that we could not leave. In the process of examining our baggage, they found some of Lucille's printed pajama patterns from the States. While waiting for the baby to be born in Xichang, Lucille had busied herself by making pajamas for the two boys.

The guards thought they had real evidence that we were spies when they found these patterns. They asked us to point out on these "maps" the location of Xichang, Lugu, and other places. Lucille couldn't help but laugh as she took pieces of the pattern and held them up against one of the guards, saying, "This is an arm. This is a leg, etc." Her actions caused me to roar with laughter, but the guards didn't think it was that funny. They still believed they had damning evidence against us and wouldn't let us leave until they had consulted with the higher authorities. Furthermore, one timid little guard told my wife that she was breaking Chinese custom by traveling too soon after the birth of the baby. Custom called for mothers not to appear in public for thirty days after giving birth to a son and forty days after giving birth to a daughter.

We wasted no time in going directly to the local authorities and telling them that we had to return to Danny and Jimmy, but they insisted on the boys being brought to Xichang. After five days of frantic negotiations, we were told that we could make the trip home.

Lucille and I looked forward to resuming our work in Lugu. When we arrived there, however, we found that an anti-American sentiment had permeated the streets of our town. This all started with America's entry into the Korean War in 1950. Prior to this time, the Communists had treated the people with courtesy and kindness and seemed interested in bettering their lot and they had even allowed us to continue our work without any hindrances. This seemed to indicate that we had made the right decision to stay in Mainland China instead of heeding the American Embassy's urgent advice to flee the country.

Even the people seemed to be happy over the change in government. The Communist underground had done a very good job of getting out their propaganda, extolling the virtues of Soviet Russia and promising the people a wonderful future if they would help in the overthrow of the Nationalists. They had infiltrated the schools and universities, and even the government. My language teacher, who was also a teacher in the Lugu Middle School, revealed himself as a Communist official after the take-over. Much Later we learned that he had often gone through the papers on my desk when

I would leave my study during our sessions together. We also discovered that he was recording the names of local officials and others who paid friendly visits to our home. Some of them were jailed. One of them was our good friend Xie Wendan, the local banker, who had befriended us. This was one of the reasons why he was taken out and executed. His poor wife finally committed suicide by jumping into the river behind their home and his nine children were divided up among the neighbors.

Actually, some of our best results came after the take-over, without any Communist interference. We soon learned that even this was in the three-head policy of the new regime: (1) the nod-head policy—yes, you can do this and you can do that; (2) the shake-head policy—no, you can't do this and you can't do that; and (3) the chop-head policy—you can't do a thing because you haven't got a head left. We saw all three phases of this policy at work. Under the nod-head policy, the Communists needed time to bring in their cadres and train them, so they left us alone. Under the shake-head policy, these trained cadres were then ready to indoctrinate (brainwash) us missionaries and the common people. Under the chop-head policy, within a nine-month period of time, 17,000 of the people in our valley were led outside the gates of our towns and shot. The majority of these people were absolutely innocent of any crimes.

Soon after their arrival, the Communists destroyed all of the opium poppy fields around our town. This didn't cause any sadness on our part since our area was part of the biggest opium producing center in the world, "The Golden Triangle." The thing that really saddened us was a decree that anyone using or trading in opium would be executed immediately. I watched these poor people stand before "kangaroo courts" set up on the streets. After trials which lasted about fifteen minutes, they were executed. This slaughter of Chinese by Chinese in our area and all over China continued until we finally read in our local Xichang newspaper that over 30,000,000 people had lost their lives in this madness called "liberation."

Yes, the people of China suffered terrible persecution under their Communist enemies. Our suffering was certainly not as great as theirs, but we did have our trials and tribulations. For instance, "the commissioners began trying to find a ground of accusation against Daniel (Daniel Carr, that is)."

"ME? A MISSIONARY?"

Chapter 19

"THE COMMISSIONERS BEGAN TRYING TO FIND A GROUND OF ACCUSATION AGAINST DANIEL"

"Then the commissioners and satraps began trying to find a ground of accusation against Daniel in regard to government affairs ..." (Daniel 6:4)

I wish I could have been as bold as the Prophet Daniel when he faced all the commissioners and satraps (lesser officials) who were trying to find a ground of accusation against him. I must confess, however, that I was more than a little uneasy when the commissioners and satraps of Communist China began bringing charges against me.

The accusations started within the first week of our liberation. All people owning firearms and radios were ordered to turn them over immediately to the government. It so happened that I did have in my possession a Colt automatic which the Navy had issued to me during the war when I was still a chaplain in the Philippines. Since the Japanese didn't respect chaplains, the Navy thought it wise to arm its chaplains with carbine rifles and Colt automatic revolvers. Even though we had no intentions of ever using them, they were still part of our official equipment.

Before being hospitalized back to the United States, I asked Ed Bomm, a missionary with the Association of Baptists for World Evangelism, to remove all the arms from my gear and turn them over to the Navy and send the rest of my gear to the China Inland Mission in Shanghai since we had already been accepted as missionaries to China with the Conservative Baptist Foreign Mission Society. Ed Bomm and his wife had been rescued from a Japanese prison camp by American troops and were suffering from beriberi. I had taken them under my wings and fattened them up on choice steaks and milkshakes at our officers' club in Manila.

Unfortunately, Ed found the carbine and turned it in but didn't find the other gun with a lot of ammunition and the shoulder belt for the carbine. When we finally reached Shanghai as missionaries, we picked up the gear that Ed had sent to the C.I.M. and included it in our freight going out to West China. You can imagine how surprised we were when we opened up our freight and found this arsenal. The only time I ever used it was in Xichang to kill a sick goat that belonged to the John Simpsons. I felt like public enemy number one as I stood there in front of that poor old goat, pointed the gun between its eyes at a distance of two feet, closed my eyes, and fired. I missed. I fired again and missed. On the third try, I was finally successful. The only other time that gun was used was when Lucille was alone with the children in Lugu. I thought I had done a good job of showing her how to use it before going with Ralph Covell on an evangelistic trip. I told her that the only time she was to use the gun was if someone tried to break into our home. She was not to fire at anybody. She was only to fire into the air to scare them off. Well, it just so happened that she heard prowlers one night, so she poked the gun out of the door and fired into the air. Apparently this scared the intruders away for no more noises were heard.

The next morning, she removed the magazine from the Colt as I had taught her. The children were sitting around her when she was performing this operation. Thinking that all the bullets were out of the gun, she pulled the trigger. POW! A bullet shot out of the chamber, missing Danny by about a foot, and buried itself in the wall. This was quite a shattering experience and Lucille was still shaking when I returned a few days later. Unfortunately, I had forgotten to tell her that after removing the magazine there would still be a bullet left in the firing chamber to be ejected.

It was this gun that I turned over to the officials in Lugu, telling them how it happened to be in my home. The radio that we had in our possession was another matter. It was a little battery-operated radio set that we had purchased in a local store while still living under the Nationalists. It was our only link with the outside world and every night we faithfully listened to the Voice of America news broadcast originating in Taiwan.

Several weeks before we bought this radio my language teacher asked my wife if we had a radio. Mistaking "radio" for "phonograph," she answered, "Yes." Later, he asked Ralph if we had a radio and Ralph honestly told him that we did not have one.

After our liberation, we reported to the officials that we had a gun and radio. When my language teacher who was now a

"THE COMMISSIONERS BEGAN ..." 185

Communist official heard about this, he naturally thought Ralph had been lying to him about our not having a radio and encouraged his cohorts to confiscate our radio. When Ralph objected to this and told them to show him the law prohibiting the ownership of a radio, they were unable to do it. The law only prohibited the possession of telegraph and sending sets. Of course these unsophisticated officials undoubtedly thought that our radio was a sending set. They were even convinced that our typewriters were sending sets and wanted us to show them how they worked. It was the Communist policy to send their backward and less qualified officials out into the rural areas where they couldn't do too much harm.

The question concerning our radio was finally resolved when the officials agreed to Ralph's suggestion that they seal the radio and leave it in our possession until they had time to confer with higher officials about the final disposition of the case. This they did by pasting a paper seal on the back of a piece of writing paper with lines on it and finally pasting it to the back of the radio after tucking in all of the battery wires. This meant that we were no longer able to receive any word from the outside.

This I didn't like, so I decided to carefully remove the seal, lead the battery wires through a knob hole in the front of the radio, and then replace the seal. If the officials came to check on the radio, I could quickly poke the battery wires back into the set and they wouldn't know the difference. To carry out this plan, I went down to the local stationery store and bought some paper which I thought looked like the paper on the back of the radio. However, when I got home and compared it with the paper bearing the seal I found that the lines were not far enough apart.

After going back to town and searching without success for matching paper, I wrote a letter to Bill Simons in Xichang. I enclosed a sample of the paper I had bought and asked him to look for paper with wider lines. Of course I couldn't tell him why I wanted the paper since all of our incoming and outgoing letters were being censored. I only said that it was very important that we receive the right paper. I often wondered what the censors made of this strange request. The paper Bill sent back was still not wide enough between the lines. I wrote him once again and told him to send paper with still wider lines. He finally found what we wanted and sent it to us with the comment, "What's going on up there in Lugu?" I'm sure if he had known, he would have had second thoughts about participating in this grand deception of the People's Republic of China.

Late one night I carefully removed the paper with its seal from the back of the radio. I slowly peeled off the seal from the old paper, pasted it on the new paper, and then pasted the new paper on the back of the radio. Unfortunately, in the process I tore a part of the seal and that could not be replaced. Well, that was something we'd just have to live with in our risky attempt to get the latest news.

I placed the precious radio in a little storage closet near my study. Each night when the half-hour news broadcast came in over the air from Taiwan, Ralph or I would go into the closet and listen to the news while the other went outside to see if any spies might be prowling around on the outside. Lucille played loudly on our little organ to drown out the noise of the radio. We always made sure that the cook had gone home and that Danny was asleep before listening to the broadcast for that young son of mine would have done quite a job of broadcasting on his own. He undoubtedly would have told the cook and everybody else who came to see us that we had a radio.

It was fortunate that our property was outside the walls of town, for it made it rather difficult for the cadres to keep check on us. They did, however, tell the boys who watched the water buffalo grazing on the land in front of our property to keep their eyes on us and report any strange doings by the foreigners.

The strange doings didn't take place until after dark. One night as I was sitting in my closet listening to the news I noticed little flecks of paper on the shelf in back of the radio. When I pulled the radio out to check on it, I noticed rat dirt all over the shelf. Apparently the rats had been attracted to the paste I had used on the seal and gnawed away on the seal which I had already torn some time before. After an initail pang of concern, it occurred to me that we now had an excuse, albeit tenuous, for the broken seal. Considering the matter even further, I decided that the best defense was a good offense and marched to town with an appropriate air of self-righteousness, carrying the radio under my arm. Though I'm not certain the officials were overly impressed with my account of the bandit seal-eating rats—afterall it was a mighty big bite—they did reseal the radio and return it to me with stern warnings to take better care of it.

The carbine belt that found its way to West China also brought some trying hours. In the midst of one of their many searches of our home, the officials found it and asked me to turn over to them the carbine itself. They wouldn't listen to my explanation of how the belt had gotten mixed up with our other belongings and threatened to imprison me if I didn't turn in the gun. This began a series of demands for the gun. Finally, an order came for me to appear on a certain day before the top official, Mr. He (Mr. Black). It just so happened that I was sick that day and Lucille went down in my place. Mr. He told her that they knew I had a carbine and they knew where the carbine was and if I didn't turn it in immediately, I would be jailed. She looked the man right in the eye and said, "You know that's a lie!"

When Lucille came home and told me that she had called Mr. He a liar, I was horrified. No one accuses Communist officials of being liars. Ralph got into serious trouble one day when he told some soldiers that they didn't know what they were talking about. They read him off in no uncertain terms and told him that if he didn't apologize, they would take him to the authorities in Xichang. If no action was taken against him there, they'd take him to provincial headquarters and, if no action was taken there, they'd take him all the way to Beijing for the final answer. Needless to say, Ralph apologized.

Now you can understand my anxiety when Lucille told me that she had called the ranking local official a liar. Fully expecting the soldiers to arrive at any moment, I told Lucille to get my sleeping bag and a few things together for a stay in prison. But no soldiers came and, strangely, the Communists never again questioned us about the carbine. Mr. He probably reasoned that if Mrs. Carr had the courage to call him a liar, she must have been telling the truth.

The intimidation by the Communists continued. Anti-American slogans were posted all over the town. Soldiers nailed to our chapel wall a large sign reading, "Oppose American Imperialism for Invading Korea and Formosa." Parades and demonstrations were plentiful and we usually stayed away from them. Propaganda leaflets were spread all over the town. Fortunately, many of the people in our town refused to believe the propaganda and claimed that we were their friends and were there to help them.

The friendliness of the soldiers soon changed to contempt and arrogance. They would even walk right into our street chapel and condemn us for saying that Jesus Christ is the greatest leader of all. I recall the time I was preaching in our Lugu street chapel when a soldier marched right down the aisle and shouted, "Do you mean to stand there and tell us that Jesus Christ is greater than our leader, Mao Zedong?" I was immediately inspired to lead the congregation in some loud singing until the man walked out. This interference on the part of the military and the cadres became part of our daily routine.

On another occasion, children attending one of our children's meetings were frightened when soldiers came in, asked them about what we had been teaching them, wrote down their names and addresses, and told them it would be best if they stayed away from our chapel. Lucille took the soldiers outside the chapel and pointed to the sign they had posted on the building which included the words, "Freedom of Religion." They sneeringly retorted, "Yes, but not for you!" One boy was so frightened that he didn't show up at his home until many hours later. His parents were worried and had gone out looking for him.

Four soldiers, members of a propaganda team, came up to our compound one day and asked me if they could use the little Estey portable organ in our chapel for an outdoor propaganda meeting that night. My answer was "No" since we needed to use it in our mid-week service that same night. Some time later, I went down to the chapel and was told by our evangelist that he had turned the organ over to four soldiers who came to him with a note from their commanding officer saying that I had given them permission to use the organ. I immediately sought Ralph's help in recovering the organ. Being a very charitable person, Ralph was inclined to let them use the organ. He wasn't overly impressed with my argument that if you gave them an inch they'd take a mile. However, when I insisted on taking some real action, he finally said, "Well, I'll go with you if you keep your big mouth shut and let me do the talking." That seemed fair enough.

When we arrived at headquarters, Ralph went up to the commanding officer and said in a very quiet tone, "Four of your men did wrong by ..." That's about all he was able to say. The officer cut him off and shouted, "How dare you say that a Communist soldier can do wrong." Needless to say, the diplomatic initiative only deteriorated after those opening remarks.

Concluding that Ralph wasn't making any progress and having promised not to speak, I picked up the little organ which had been placed next to the officer's desk, put it on my shoulder, brushed aside a soldier who was pointing a gun at me, and simply carried the organ back to our street chapel.

When Ralph didn't show up at the chapel, I decided to go back and check on him. When he saw me enter the room, he shouted, "It's about time you came back. They were holding me until you returned." To make the story short, we were not released until Ralph apologized for insulting the entire Communist army and I apologized for stealing Communist property. In the end, we had won the battle. The organ was safely back in the chapel for the evening service.

Many of us working in China felt that democracy could never succeed as a viable political system in China until the literacy rate could be raised dramatically. Few adults could read and write. The Communists were also aware of this fact. It is always easier to indoctrinate an educated person than an ignorant one, especially if you monopolize all of the sources of information. The Communists set about to educate the populace through street propaganda meetings and "group therapy" sessions. These periods of discussion and confession often resulted in testimony meetings on the streets and reports of these confessions in the local newspapers. Perfect frankness was emphasized in these confessions in order that the others might help them "recover" from the shock of living under the corrupt Nationalist regime.

The homes in our town were divided into cells of ten homes each. At least one member from each family had to attend these indoctrination classes. At the end of each session an examination was given. If anyone flunked the examination, he was punished in one way or another and often sent to jail. It was important that these family representatives learn their lessons well, for they had the big responsibility of indoctrinating all the other members of the family.

It wasn't necessary for secret police, so common in the former regime, to monitor the "brain-washing" that went on in our community. Each political cadre spent most of his time watching over his cell, entering homes without knocking at any time of the day or night. There was also the "watch-care" offered by the neighbors, and even other members of the family. It is customary in China for family members to take their arguments out on the streets for the neighbors to settle. Everyone knows everyone else's business.

With all of the self-study groups taking place and confessions being made, anyone opposing the party line would immediately be reported, often by members of his own family and especially by the children who were kept in school from morning to night, seven days a week, and taught that to be good Communists they had a duty to report even the faults of their own fathers and mothers. How shocked we were one day when we noticed a crowd of people standing in front of a home across the street from our chapel. The parents were being led off to jail because of the testimony of their own children.

Many of the accused were sent off to re-education camps where daily "brain-washing" sessions and hard labor reshaped their thinking before they returned to society. With "comrades" at their sides, their words and actions were checked. Many of them tried to impress their comrades by openly denouncing the United States and the former regime even though there were certainly big questions in their minds about the new government.

The local merchants and landlords were bemoaning their new lot. Under the Nationalists they had never paid real taxes. It had been the poor farmers who paid because they couldn't hide their grain and were too poor to bribe the tax collector. Now the landlords had to pay taxes, not in money but in grain. They would have been happy to sell or give away their land, but now property ownership could not be changed in light of a new land policy which was being formulated.

The common people were also bewildered. They had been told by the officials that the land would be taken from the rich and given to them. Many of the people turned against their landlords and reported their "crimes" to the local militia. Owning just a few acres of land could cause a person to be branded a hated landlord. I remember standing on the main street of town and watching soldiers dragging landlords into town. The soldiers were on horseback and the landlords were running along behind with ropes tied around their necks. They were soon standing before a pick-up "kangaroo court" and summarily sentenced to death. How shocked I was when a woman picked up a club and beat her convicted landlord over the the head until he fell unconscious in the dust. When he regained consciousness, they marched him out to the execution grounds which were not far from our home and shot him.

It wasn't long before landlords were a thing of the past. While it's true that the landlords lost their land, the land was not given to the common people as promised. It became the property of the state. We couldn't even cut down a tree on our land without government approval. The people were simply assigned a piece of land and told to work it from sunrise to sunset or go to jail.

Those without land parcels were told to go out and find work at once or be jailed. A few hours after this order went out, a number of people appeared at our gate, some crying, and asked if they could work our unused land. They mentioned the new order and we were glad to grant their request. Not surprisingly, the government was soon collecting taxes on the crops produced by these people. Two thirds of their produce had to be given to the government in taxes and they were to live on the remaining one-third. This was a far worse arrangement than when they had share-cropped with their landlords. They had become little more than slaves of the new state.

Our national evangelist was told that Christian work was not productive and was ordered to go out and find a productive job. He was to work seven days a week from sunrise to sunset. Not knowing anything about farming and having had only Bible school training, he turned despairingly to selling stockings on street corners. How our hearts went out to him and his family. We tried to teach him how to make soap and sell it for a living, but our attempt failed when we were unable to make soap from the directions contained in a less that helpful "survival" handbook.

Our Christians were accused of collaborating with missionary spies from the West who were supporting American troops in their war against Chinese troops in Korea. To protect themselves, some of them began condemning us publicly in the hope of convincing the officials that Christians were patriotic Chinese. The same was true in other parts of China. These Christians became very vocal on the issue and we could understand why. Undoubtedly many of them were afraid that Christianity might be banned completely and they felt that they had to take this public position in order to save the Church in China. Others might have done this out of fear for their lives.

Over and over again the people heard the same old line that religion was nothing more than an opiate of the masses and necessary for the survival of democratic systems. Under Communism, however, there was no need for the opiate and the Christian literature that Chinese and foreign Christians had been passing out all over China. This kind of literature was branded as self-centered, other worldly, and pietistic escapism. Despite this harangue, the government allowed the Church to continue its ministry. After all, the people had been guaranteed religious freedom under Article 88 of the Communist Constitution.

The Chinese Communists were trying to redesign every part of the social order and, to that end, tried to use Christianity as another tool in their effort. Churches were permitted to remain open only so long as it was thought they would serve their purpose in establishing a state grounded in materialistic atheism. Church leaders had to break all ties with churches outside of China and bow to the supervision and control of atheistic officials. They had to avoid any activity that might bring shame to the government.

In order to guarantee the cooperation of the church, government officials sat down with forty well-known Protestant church leaders in July 1950 and helped them in the establishment of the "Three-Self Reform Movement" (often called the "Three-Self Movement") and in the publication of a "Christian Manifesto" ("The Direction of Endeavor for Chinese Christianity in the Construction of the New China") which reads:

> *Protestant Christianity has been introduced to China for more than 140 years. During this period it has made not an unworthy contribution to Chinese society. Nevertheless, and this was most unfortunate, not long after Christianity's coming to China, imperialism started its activities here; and since the principle groups of missionaries who brought Christianity to China all came themselves from these imperialistic countries, Christianity consciously or unconsciously, directly or indirectly, became related with imperialism.*
>
> *Now that the Chinese revolution has achieved victory, these imperialistic countries will not rest passively content in face of this unprecedented historical fact in China. They will certainly seek to contrive by every means the destruction of what has actually been achieved; they may also make use of Christianity to forward their plot of stirring up internal dissension, and creating reactionary forces in this country.*
>
> *It is our purpose in publishing the following statement to heighten our vigilance against imperialism, to make clear the political stand of Christians in New China, to hasten the building of a Chinese church whose affairs are managed by the Chinese themselves, and to indicate the responsibilities that should be taken up by Christians throughout the whole country in national reconstruction in New China. We desire to call upon all Christians in the country to exert their best efforts in putting into effect the principles presented.*

The Task in General

Christian churches and organizations give thoroughgoing support to the "Common Political Platform," and under the leadership of the government oppose imperialism, feudalism, and bureaucratic capitalism, and take part in the effort to build an independent, democratic, peaceable, unified, prosperous, and powerful New China.

Fundamental Aims

1. Christian churches and organizations in China should exert their utmost efforts, and employ effective methods, to make people in the churches everywhere recognize clearly the evils that have been wrought in China by imperialism; recognize the fact that in the past imperialism has made use of Christianity itself; and be vigilant against imperialism, and especially American imperialism, in its plot to use religion in fostering the growth of reactionary forces. At the same time, the churches and organizations should call upon Christians to participate in the movement opposing war and upholding peace, and teach them thoroughly to understand and support the government's policy of agrarian reform.

2. Christian churches and organizations in China should take effective measures to cultivate a patriotic and democratic spirit among their adherents in general, as well as a psychology of self-respect and self-reliance. The movement of autonomy, self-support, and self-propagation hitherto promoted in the Chinese church has already attained a measure of success. This movement from now onward should complete its tasks within the shortest possible period. At the same time, self-criticism should be advocated, all forms of Christian activity reexamined and readjusted, and thorough-going austerity measures adopted, so as to achieve the goals of a reformation in the church.

Concrete Methods

1. *All Christian churches and organizations in China that are still relying upon foreign personnel and financial aid should work out concrete plans to realize within the shortest possible time their objective of self-reliance and rejuvenation.*

2. *From now onward, as regards their religious work, Christian churches and organizations should lay emphasis upon a deeper understanding of the nature of Christianity itself, closer fellowship and unity among the various denominations, the cultivation of better leadership personnel, and reform in systems of church organization. As regards their more general work, they should emphasize anti-imperialistic, anti-feudalistic and anti-bureaucratic-capitalistic education, together with such forms of service to the people as productive labor, teaching them to understand the New Era, cultural and recreational activities, literacy education, medical and public health work, and care of children.*

The signing of this "Christian Manifesto" by our Christians and Christians all over China ushered in the "Three-Self Reform Movement" for Protestant churches in New China. The Church was to be self-governing, self-supporting, and self-propagating. How ironic it was that the Communists should introduce a religious policy that many missionaries desired but had never realized. There were certain elements in this manifesto which evoked much heart searching on the part of missionaries in China and missionaries all over the world.

Many restrictions were placed upon us after the manifesto was signed. Mr. He was quick to inform us that we could no longer work in the rural areas and that we would have to stop our work among the mountain tribes. We were to confine our efforts to the streets of Lugu. Fewer people were coming to our chapel services. On the other hand, they did continue to come to our dispensary for treatment, some from long distances away.

We sat down with our faithful Chinese co-laborers and asked their opinion about the state of things. They were the ones who had

"THE COMMISSIONERS BEGAN ..."

really born the brunt of public criticism and scorn for continuing to work with the American imperialists. Their advice was for us to take it easy for awhile and let them do the preaching in the chapel. The good thing about it was that during this period of time a number of people did take a greater interest in the Gospel of Jesus Christ and found it much better than the Gospel of Communism. The work continued on a fairly steady level until the publication of the "Christian Manifesto" in December of 1950.

In January 1951, my wife and I included the following in our final letter from the mainland of China to our mission board in the States:

> *God in His good pleasure has seen fit to bring our work in China to a close. Instead of questioning His will in the matter, we are simply praying that He might steady our hearts and hush any sound of regret. Certainly He has a purpose in it all. Our position out here has been made untenable by the following announcement:*
>
> *1. An announcement by the Executive Yuan of the Central Chinese People's Government, dated December 29, 1950, of the regulations for the registration of cultural, educational, and charitable organizations (including church bodies) receiving foreign aid or depending upon foreign funds. (This announcement takes the work out of our hands and places it in the hands of the government). Each registered organization, after it has definitely severed its connection with foreign countries, may request the People's Government to cancel its registration.*
>
> *2. An announcement that religious organizations and church members all over China have signed a "Christian Manifesto" (drawn up by the Church in China) calling for a complete break with all foreign mission societies and missionary personnel.*
>
> *3. An announcement by the Executive Yuan on December 28, 1950, that: (a) All property of the American Government and American business enterprises (including mission organizations) should immediately be controlled*

by the local People's Government, and moreover be investigated clearly; (b) American public and private bank deposits within the People's Republic of China should immediately be frozen.

Number three makes it imperative that we leave the country as soon as possible. Our property has already been investigated and most of our equipment has been sealed, and our funds have been frozen. We would ask you to pray much about this matter of funds. From a human standpoint, the situation is critical. Nothing more in the way of funds can be sent us from the States. And even if our frozen funds are returned to us, they will not be enough to cover a decent exodus out of China. And from this amount must also come our living expenses from now until the time permission is given us to leave.

We're praising the Lord that we don't have to look at things from a human standpoint. We're claiming Romans 8:28 like we've never claimed it before: "And we know that all things work together for good to them that love God, to them who are the called according to his purpose."

The government took immediate steps to carry out the orders mentioned above. On January 16, 1951 the Public Security Bureau went to all of our stations and made a complete search of our belongings. It was unfortunate that I had forgotten to turn over to the local officials a second box of bullets for the gun that I had already given to them. I had meant to throw them into the river near our home; but this I neglected to do. Now men from the Security Bureau were knocking on our gate. My immediate reaction was to dump the bullets into our Nanking heater which was located in our little bathroom in a loft just above our kitchen stove. Our heater was nothing more than a fifty-gallon steel drum with a smaller drum cemented into it. Circulating in the gap between the two drums was hot air from the flu of our wood-burning kitchen stove down below. Our bathtub was not a luxurious stateside model. It was one-half of a fifty-gallon drum set up on wooden blocks, making it impossible for us to stretch out and enjoy a real soaking. It was also quite rough on our backs.

"THE COMMISSIONERS BEGAN ..."

After dumping the bullets in the smaller drum which held our hot water, I covered them with a weighted pan, thinking that the searchers would probably poke around in the drum of water. I also told my wife to rush up to the bathroom and start giving the children a bath in the hope the men would feel too embarrassed to enter the room while it was being used. But there was no such reticence on their part and they entered the room. One man poked around in the drum with a long stick since the water was too hot for him to put his hands in it.

Not finding anything in the bathroom, they proceeded to the other rooms in the house and sealed our camera and other equipment. They made two lists of everything they had confiscated, giving us one list and keeping the other. They also made us sign a statement that they had treated us with courtesy during the search. After they left, Ralph and I scooped out the bullets and carried them out to a little shed in our yard, accompanied, of course, by the loud playing of Lucille on the organ. After digging a deep hole, we buried the bullets. I wonder if they are still there.

The harassment continued. On one of their many searches, they lined us up against a wall, poked their bayonets at our stomachs, and threatened to kill us. We tried to comfort the children by telling them that the soldiers were just kidding us and wouldn't do us any harm. How it grieved our hearts to see our children undergoing this long period of mental torment. We were especially concerned about Jimmy. During the year and a half that we were in Communist hands, Jimmy came down with a strange fever that just wouldn't go away. Every day his termperature was high. Medical experts were no longer available to us and the officials wouldn't let us take him out of the country. He ached in every joint in his body and often we could do nothing to ease his pain but carry him around. Added to his fever was the ongoing trauma of Communist harassment.

Prior to this fever, Jimmy had been a very brave, happy, and friendly little boy. He was speaking very fluently and had no trouble learning. But after this fever came upon him and after such awful treatment at the hands of the Reds, he retreated into a shell and has never come out of it. He became like a frightened little animal and refused to leave his mother's side. When we finally did come out of China and had Jimmy examined by specialists in the States, we were told that he had undoubtedly suffered from rheumatic fever and that his heart and brain had been damaged. We were also told that if we had been able to bring him out sooner, they could have treated him and probably prevented the brain damage. But the Communists would not allow us to leave, so we had to stay and suffer more indignities at their hands.

Our colleagues in our other stations were going through equally as many trials and tribulations as we. On the day that all of our stations were searched, men from the Security Bureau in Xichang searched the home of our Field Director, Dr. Lee Lovegren. They found in his possession one of his old army uniforms, some old Army maps of the area, and some detailed weather readings that he had been preparing for the National Geographic Society of which he was a member. With this evidence in hand, they accused him of being a spy for the American Strategic Services, an intelligence agency that was the predecessor to the Central Intelligence Agency. While it was true that during World War II Lee had been an officer in China with the Office of Strategic Services, he was not an operative and simply served as an interpreter for the agency. Local officials had gone to a lot of trouble to build up a case agaist Lee. First, there was an accusation meeting in which people were asked to make charges against him, but he was unable to answer these charges since he was not allowed to attend that part of the meeting. Then he was brought into the meeting hall where he was asked to talk about the work of the American Strategic Services. Not realizing what had gone on in the earlier part of the meeting, Lee gave a detailed report on this work. After he had finished, the officials told the people that Lee had just made a confession of his spy activities. It wasn't until then that Lee realized that he had been tricked.

Though the charges against him were false, the report that Lee gave and the documents which were found in his house proved damaging at a time when America and China were at war. The home of the Lovegrens was sealed and Lee was led off to Yaan, the capital city of Xikang Province. His wife, Ida, was allowed to go with him and lived in a little Chinese inn while he was imprisoned in Yaan for several years. She was allowed to visit him. Later he was transferred to a prison in Chungking and Ida found it necessary to go on to Hong Kong to wait for him to come out of China. Fortunately, her daughter Mildred, a Southern Baptist missionary stationed in Hong Kong, was there to keep her company while they waited for Lee to one day join them.

Lee was constantly questioned by interrogation teams, indoctrinated with Marxist teachings, and advised to sign a confession. All their attempts at "brain-washing" Lee failed. If he had been willing to sign a confession, he probably would have been released earlier and ordered out of China. But Lee was a hardheaded Swede and a strong Christian. He was not going to confess to something that he did not do. That would have been a lie, and lying was against his principles. It was four years before he was allowed to join his wife in Hong Kong. While waiting for Lee, Ida carried on a fine ministry among refugees from mainland China.

Lee's arrest dealt a hard blow to our Xichang Church. The members were accused of supporting his "spy" activities, our chapel was closed, and the members were told they could only attend services at the Border Service Church. This church had joined the government-supported Three-Self Church organization.

While all of this was going on in Xichang, we were still fighting a "battle" in Lugu. A number of people came to our compound after finding out that we were trying to leave China. Some were welcomed and others were not. The former came via the door and the latter via the wall. A couple of good watchdogs discouraged those coming over the wall but not those coming through it. Those trying to come through the wall were probably Nosu tribespeople who scorned the orthodox way of entering our house and adopted the burrowing policy of a mole—an old Nosu trick. Providentially they struck the back of a heavy wooden shelf attached to our inner wall and mistook it for a wooden barrier sunk in the wall and their efforts resulted in nothing more than a gaping hole in our tamped mud wall. The damage was easily repaired with the splashing on of more mud. The rear wall of our residence was actually the east wall of our compound. Our dogs and that old wooden shelf thwarted three attempts to enter our compound within a period of three weeks. The Lord uses some mighty strange instruments to watch over His own.

Practically everybody in our little town knew we were planning to leave and some had decided that this was a good time to make a haul. Others came to say goodbye and were really sorry over the prospect of our leaving. Several of our Nosu friends came with a jug of wine to help say farewell and seemed quite disappointed when we had to refuse a farewell drink. They seemed genuinely sorry that we were planning to leave. We were sorry, too, when we thought of the many in our area who had never had the opportunity to hear of Jesus and His love. But God was much more concerned over their spiritual welfare than we and if He chose to remove us from the field, He certainly had other and better plans for them. How wonderful it was to have the confidence that through it all He was working out His perfect will!

The Covells and we decided that the cheapest way out was to hire two or three horses for our baggage and walk some three hundred miles over the mountains to Yaan in the north. We rigged up a contraption for carrying Marilyn Jean, now six months of age, on our backs. Lucille tried to ready herself for the trip by spending some time each day carrying Marilyn around on her back. We were certain that for an extra fee Danny and Jimmy could find a perch on the backs of the men handling our horses. Rafts, trucks and boats would provide our transportation from Yaan to a port on the east coast of China. At the time, we thought that Shanghai would be that port. But the best laid plans of mice and men often go astray. So it was in our case.

On February 13, 1951, Ralph was ordered to appear before an officer of the Public Security Bureau and was told that he was to be expelled from China for taking some pictures of opium fields several years before under the Nationalist regime. He was told to write a confession and have it printed in the local paper for a period of seven days. If no one accused him of anything during that period of time, he and Ruth would be escorted out of China. What a jolt this was to all of us. We were not going to leave the country together as we had planned. Our ministry and blessed fellowship with the Covells in West China had come to a very sad end. Ralph did write a letter of confession and it was published in the newspaper for seven days. When no accusations were made against him, three soldiers with fixed bayonets led Ralph and Ruth out of Lugu on February 28, 1951, and escorted them on the first stage of their journey out of China.

At about this same time, Mr. He and a group of soldiers escorted us to Xichang where we were placed under house arrest with the Simons and the Simpsons. We settled down in the little two-room adobe house that the Staffords had occupied before returning to the United States because of sickness in the family. Bill and Flossie Simons were very kind in asking us to have our meals with them. We, along with our fellow missionaries in Huili, had already asked for permission to leave the country. All we could do was to be patient and wait for the government to grant that permission.

In the meantime, we were totally isolated from the church members in town. Our presence on the field was a real threat to them and the basis for continual harsh accusations of collaborating with missionary spies from the West who were supporting American troops in the their war against Chinese troops in Korea. One member was jailed because of his friendship with us missionaries. He finally persuaded a sympathetic guard to give us a note in which he sadly apologized for taking his own life because he was no longer able to stand the torture.

The common people were still being whipped into line by their Red masters. Many of them were made to join "slave-labor" teams. The order would go out that each family had to provide one laborer, sometimes more, to work on a public project for a day and sometimes for six months without any pay—all for the glory of the new regime. I must confess that they worked wonders with these labor teams—new public roads, bridges, parks, etc. If a family had no male laborer to provide, then a woman would have to go out and work. We would often see these teams passing by our house under fixed bayonets. Included among them were women with little babies strapped to their backs.

Even we missionaries had to share in these projects even though the government would often allow us to get out of work if we paid a small fee amounting to about a quarter in American money. Most of the ordinary people were unable to buy their way out of work since their average monthly salary at that time amounted to not more than the equivalent of four or five dollars in American money.

I recall one time when we were unable to buy our way out of work. It was on a Sunday morning when we were just about ready to have devotions on our compound. A troop of soldiers came on to our compound and saw me standing there with Bill Simons. They ordered us to go out and sweep the street in front of our residence. I told them that the street didn't belong to us and if they wanted it swept they would have to sweep it themselves. Without another word, the officer in charge lifted his bayonet and the others lifted theirs and told us to move. Well, we moved. We were marched out to the street where we started sweeping while a number of off-duty soldiers sat alongside the road and laughed and pointed their fingers at us. We spent the rest of the day sweeping that street, for just as soon as we completed sweeping it another military horse train would come through and we'd have to repeat the process all over again.

It seemed as though I was always pulling one blooper after another. I remember the time I was standing in our Xichang compound when I heard the sound of machine-gun fire. The rear wall of our compound was also part of the wall around our town. The local garrison would often have machine-gun practice on the other side of the wall and sometimes we would make our way up to the top of the wall and watch them. On this occasion, I went up to see the action. However, when I arrived there, not one soldier was to be seen even though the sound of gunfire could still be heard. A few minutes later, four soldiers with fixed bayonets appeared on top of the wall and led me off to military headquarters. Communist soldiers were always displaying their bayonets in order to impress

"THE COMMISSIONERS BEGAN ..." 205

the people with their toughness. As I marched along with them on all four sides of me, I noticed that other soldiers were rushing through the streets with rifles and small mortars. Apparently they thought a large group of Nationalist stragglers with the help of some Nosu tribespeople were trying to retake the town and that I had been signaling to them from the top of the wall.

I was placed for a short period of time in a cell guarded by four soldiers. While they waited for the officers in charge to arrive, I stood at the bars of my cell listening to their conversation. I heard one guard say to another guard in a voice loud enough for me to hear, "I wonder if we'll take this missionary out today and shoot him or wait until tomorrow." I tried to settle their question by telling them to shoot me right then, for they'd be doing me a big favor by helping me reach my Heavenly Home. Of course they thought I was crazy for making such a strange request. After all, the death threat was their main way of keeping the people under control. Actually, it was a wonderful opportunity to testify to them about the matter of life and death.

I was soon questioned by those in command and released. Even when we make mistakes, God mercifully brings us through. In my case, it was a sympathetic Communist official who recognized me as being one of those missionaries who had stayed in his inn while he was chief of police in Mianning under the old government. You will recall that Ralph Covell and I had been bothered by the sound of gambling in his inn when we stayed there for a number of days during an evangelistic campaign. How grateful I was for his remembering me and persuading the other officials to release me. God often uses a "crooked stick" to perform His wonders. He did it for the Prophet Daniel when he gained the sympathy of the pagan King Darius and assured him that he was still alive in the lions' den by shouting out to him, "My God shut the lions' mouths ... I was found innocent ..."

Chapter 20

"I WAS FOUND INNOCENT"

> *"Then Daniel spoke to the king, 'O king, live forever! My God sent His angel and shut the lions' mouths, and they have not harmed me, inasmuch as I was found innocent before Him; and also toward you, O king, I have committed no crime.'" (Daniel 6:21,22)*

I can now understand in a small way how the Prophet Daniel felt when he declared his innocence to King Darius who was so relieved when he discovered that Daniel had not been devoured by the lions. Thanks to the testimony of that sympathetic Communist official, I was found innocent of the crime of aiding and abetting the enemy. Just a few weeks before, he and several other officials had come to our home to question us about our missionary activities. What a shock he received when he recognized me. In the hope that I wouldn't show any recognition of him, he was the loudest and most obnoxious of our questioners. When he was leaving our house, he gave me a furtive and grateful smile. I gave him that same smile a few weeks later when he convinced his cohorts that I was innocent of trying to help the enemy seize the town.

Though it was nice to be declared innocent by a few Communist officials, I soon discovered that this kind of clemency was short lived when I was escorted home and informed that I would remain under house arrest until all the people of Xichang also declared me innocent. This decision by the populace was a long time in coming. We were required to post a notice in the local newspaper for a number of days stating that we were seeking permission to leave the country and that if any of the people had complaints or claims against us they were to notify the local officials. For instance, they could make false claims that we owed them money and all we could do was pay them through the officials who handled our money. Any attempt on our part to contest these complaints meant a longer delay in receiving our permission to leave.

The principal reason for detaining us longer than other missionaries was because we were under greater suspicion. Unlike those missionaries who were at liberty to move freely about their town, we were confined to our compound because they suspected us of being accomplices of Lee Lovegren. Furthermore, they discovered that Bill Simons and I had been chaplains with the Seventh Fleet during World War II. At that time the Seventh Fleet was deployed off China's east coast and they suspected that we were still in the U.S. Navy and spying for the Seventh Fleet just as they suspected Lovegren of still being a U.S. Army intelligence officer.

The only thing we could do was to wait as they tried to build up a cast against us. We tried to keep ourselves busy by attending to the daily routine of carrying water to keep our large earthenware jars filled, making fires, boiling water, scrubbing clothes over our crude outside clay fire-bed, washing diapers, purifying sugar, buying food from local vendors, cooking, teaching the Calvert Kindergarten Course to the two eldest children on the compound, stuffing up rat holes, only to see the rats glaring at us out of other holes.

We also shared in daily devotions, studyied the Word, and read books left behind by American troops who had billeted in Xichang while searching for those American airmen supposedly taken captive by Nosu tribesmen. The majority of these books were mystery novels by Earle Stanley Gardner.

Letter-writing was not a part of our daily routine since all of our out-going and in-coming mail had to be censored. The careless writing of one sentence or the use of the wrong word could be held against us. The very few letters that did reach us from the States after many months on the road were so blacked-out by the censors that they made very little sense. For all practical purposes, we had lost contact with the rest of the world.

Parcheesi became a major event and the source of competitive fervor that would rival the Super Bowl. It was a lot of fun, but I did object to Flossie Simons sacrificing her own chances of winning by making certain moves to help her husband win. It was very kind and noble on her part, but it didn't help me one bit. Since Lucille and I were not so self-sacrificing and enjoyed trying to cut each other's throat by playing fo win, what chance did we have of winning when Flossie and Bill were teamed up against us.

Speaking of kindness, Flossie did reap the full benefit of my kindness when I did some work on her teeth. Since reputable dentists were not available in that part of China, I told her that I would fill one of her teeth and alleviate the pain that she had been suffering. Numbered among my medical supplies were dental tools and guttapercha to be used for temporary fillings. I did for Flossie as I had done for my wife several months before in Lugu. I scraped most of the decay out of her tooth and filled it with the temporary filling. I'm proud to say that I did relieve the pain that both Lucille and Flossie had been suffering. Of course when they finally returned to the States, their dentists told them that I had indeed killed their pain but at the same time I had killed the nerves in their teeth and the teeth had to be extracted. Lucille's dentist almost rolled on the floor with laughter when he looked at the x-ray of her tooth and asked, "Who in the world filled that tooth?" Naturally, my wife told him that I was the culprit.

Toothaches were not the only pain that our wives had to bear while we were being held in Xichang. They also had to suffer the pain of trying to feed their husbands and children. Money was needed to buy food and wood for the stove. Since the government had declared our property and the property surrounding it a restricted military area, we had no way of leaving that area to buy the bare necessities in town. Furthermore, we had no control over the funds needed to buy those necessities. All of our assets had been sealed—paper money, lumps of gold and silver, and large bolts of cotton thread. Since paper money could lose most of its value overnight due to the troubled exchange market, we kept most of our assets in the form of cotton thread which remained steady on the market. If we needed paper money to buy goods, we would exchange some thread. Our shed full of thread was now under the control of local officials. What an ordeal it was to go through the usual routine of begging the Reds to exchange our thread for currency in order that we might buy food and fuel. Invariably, they gave us less than we requested. There was also the problem of the guards not allowing vendors to come to our home in this restricted area.

Things came to a head one day when a guard prevented some men from delivering wood to our compound. Their pack train of horses was turned away. Lucille just happened to be standing at one of our windows and saw what was taking place. Filled with "righteous indignation," she rushed to the main gate of the military headquarters and reprimanded the guards for turning the horse train away. They shoved her with their bayonets and kept ordering her to return to our compound. She refused. A high-ranking officer, hearing the commotion, came to the gate to learn what the problem was. Lucille said, "We have asked permission to leave China. Since you will not grant that permission, you must allow us to buy wood. If we have no wood, we cannot cook." The officer, fearing an international incident, reprimanded the guards and allowed her to run down the hill and persuade the horse train to return. Our thread was not the only thing to be sealed in the shed on our compound. Our cameras, binoculars, typewriters, certain tools, and bicycles were also sealed. Those things which were not sealed were not to be sold or given away. The Public Security men had made a thorough search of our homes and listed everything that we had. We were made to sign a form, acknowledging the possession of these things and holding us responsible for anything that might disappear.

Throughout this long ordeal, we continued to press for permission to leave the country and to receive the all important visas to make it possible. I have already mentioned that these visas would not be granted until the people had a chance to bring charges against us. Our missionaries to the south in Huili had already gone through this long process and were allowed to leave their town the latter part of May. After five days on the road, they arrived in Xichang and were quartered for several days in our compound where the officials could keep an eye on them. What a wonderful time of fellowship we had with them and how we rejoiced with them over the securing of their exit visas. After a good rest in Xichang, they prepared to leave our town on the ninth of June. The night before their departure, I was playing the organ in the living room when Hannah Cole walked in and asked me to play her favorite song, "Beulah Land." That I was glad to do and, as I played, she sang the words:

> *O Beulah Land, sweet Beulah Land,*
> *As on the highest mount I stand,*
> *I look away across the sea,*
> *Where mansions are prepared for me,*
> *And view the shining glory shore,*
> *My Heav'n, my home forevermore.*

"I WAS FOUND INNOCENT" 213

Little did I realize as she sang that beautiful song that she would be entering Beulah Land just ten days later. The following morning, we said goodbye to our Huili missionaries and asked God's blessing upon them as they headed north to Fulin via our town of Lugu. The road was rough and steep and their carriers and horse train handlers were abusive and constantly griping about the size of their loads. The summer heat and filthy inns that they stayed in along the road and the press of people around them added to their woes. Furthermore, they knew that the area they were passing through was undergoing a severe meningitis epidemic.

When they arrived in the town of Fulin, they were given comfortable quarters at the Catholic Mission. The Catholic priest in charge was very kind to them and tried to make them feel at home. It was there that Hannah went into a coma and about four o'clock the following morning on June 19, 1951, entered that Heavenly Home she had been singing about not too many days before. She left behind her husband, George, and four small children. The youngest was still nursing. One of our missionaries, Esther Nelson, was a nurse. She had attended Hannah at the end and had to break the sad news to George and the others that Hannah had died of meningitis. How good it was that the Garrisons and the two single ladies, Esther Nelson and Flora Mae Duncan, could be there to comfort and help with the children.

Jim Garrison managed to buy an unfinished coffin from a farmer and, after receiving permission from police headquarters, was able to arrange for Hannah's burial in a plot of ground donated by the Catholic Mission. He then conducted a brief burial service and left some money with the priest to have a memorial stone placed on the grave. The following morning our little band of missionaries left Fulin and continued their long trek out of China. The priest in Fulin had told them that the incubation period of meningitis was four days and for a number of days they wondered if their aches and pains along the way meant that they had contracted the disease. Three months later on September 16, 1951, we were just getting ready to eat our lunch when soldiers suddenly rushed onto our compound with the crisp command: "You must leave today!" We were to follow the same route that the Huili party had taken. That meant traveling 2,000 miles overland by foot, horse, huagan, truck, boat, and train to Hong Kong. They turned over to us just enough money to make the trip.

Our spontaneous "Thank God!" gave way to frenzied activity. We men, with the help of the soldiers who wanted to get rid of us as quickly as possible, speedily arranged for carriers and a horse train. Since most of the horses in West China were very small and we were unable to ride them without dragging our feet on the ground, we had to find horses or mules big enough for us to ride. Huagans also had to be provided for the women and children. I had earlier taken two rattan chairs and secured them between the bamboo poles of a huagan. This made it possible for five-year-old Danny and three-year-old Jimmy to ride together, facing each other. I had also rigged up a huagan with a seat for Lucille and a wicker basket at her feet for one-year-old Marilyn.

The women also flew into action. They had long before packed some of our major necessities into duffle bags and baskets. The majority of our possessions had already been "purchased" by the government. That was when they demanded we make an exhaustive list of our possessions—furniture, bedding, dishes, kitchen equipment, typewriters, etc. Then they paid us a few dollars for the lot. This meant that they had not confiscated our things. They had purchased them.

As the women began bundling things in oil slicks for the journey, the soldiers stood around checking everything. They allowed me to take my accordion, but when Lucille tried to pack one of our two valuable Chinese possessions—a cloisonne vase—she heard again the two words we had become so accustomed to, "Bujuen! (Not permitted!)." We had heard those words during the days. We had dreamed them during the nights. At times they angered us. At times they caused us to laugh. We had heard, "Not permitted!" so long that we were hardly prepared for the order, "You must leave today!" But we were still not permitted to take our cloisonne vase with us. We were told that it was a Chinese art treasure and art treasures could not be taken out of the country.

Fortunately, Irene and Flossie had previously helped unstuff a quilt that we needed for the road and restuff it with the Nosu clothing our Nosu friends had so kindly made for us. As the ladies quickly gathered together blankets, diapers, jackets, and the barest necessities for the horse train, the soldiers kept saying, "Too much, too much." It wasn't long before the "to be left behind" pile got bigger and bigger and the "necessities" pile smaller and smaller. Flossie took the food we had not been allowed to eat at lunchtime and packed it away with other foodstuffs we had put aside for our journey.

In the midst of all the commotion, Mrs. Han—our good friend and wonderful Bible woman—was escorted onto the compound. It had been a long time since we had been able to see her or communicate with any of our Christians; then why did the officials bring her up this last day? Always scrupulous in maintaining protocol, they could not destroy or take any of our things without our signing them away or accepting some ridiculously small token payment. Something had to be done with our property papers and the Bibles, hymn books, and miscellaneous materials stored on our property when the Communists had ordered the closing of our street chapel. Mrs. Han had been ordered to pick up the things that belonged to the church. What would happen to them, we did not know.

While her escort was occupied elsewhere, Lucille managed to have a few moments alone with her in the storeroom. Unable to control her tears, she told of her sorrow. Her oldest daughter, a college student in another town, had already joined the Communist Party and wrote glorious accounts of the accomplishments of the Party and urged her parents to join the Party, too. Likewise, her two young sons were forced to attend daily indoctrination classes where they were urged to expose their parents and highly praised if they did so, so she dared not talk much about God at home lest the children be tricked into reporting and suffer because of it. But the recourse of private prayer and trust in God could not be taken from her. A quick hug and a promise to faithfully pray for her and her family was all that Lucille could manage before Mrs. Han's escort arrived and led her off of the compound.

In our rush to get away, I forgot to pack a large piece of pure jade about the size of a small egg that was in the pocket of a shirt I had left hanging on the wall. Just the day before a good friend of ours, a wealthy intellectual who had befriended us when we first arrived in Xichang several years before, slipped by the guards and sneaked to our house. He quickly gave me the jade as a going-away gift and told me that the officials were bringing charges against him and would probably execute him. The kind fellow then quickly returned to his home by safely crawling around the main gate.

How I thank God that I didn't have to crawl around gates in order to make my way back to my home in America. After leading me straight through the main gate of Xichang, "He then brought me out through the ... gate facing east."

"I WAS FOUND INNOCENT"

"ME? A MISSIONARY?"

Chapter 21

"HE THEN BROUGHT ME OUT THROUGH THE GATE FACING EAST"

"He then brought me out through the north gate and led me around the outside to the outer gate facing east ..." (Ezekiel 47:2 NIV)

How surprised Ezekiel must have been when he had that wonderful vision of the millenial kingdom with its river of healing water outside the eastern gate of Jerusalem. Our redemption from Communist China and return to the safety of America certainly wasn't as spectacular as Israel's future deliverance, but I still marvel at the way God escorted us through the gate of Xichang which led to the north and then led us for thirty one days around to that gate on the east coast of China—HONG KONG!

Our party of eight adults and ten children—ranging in age from one year to six and a half years—included three families from the Conservative Baptist Mission, Bill and a very pregnant Flossie Simons with their two children, Russell and Martha, John and Irene Simpson with Linn Ann, Jeannie, and Marjorie and Dan and Lucille Carr with Danny, Jimmy, and Marilyn, and one English Baptist family, Bill and Win Upchurch with their two children. The Upchurches had been working in Xichang with the Border Service Mission of the Church of Christ in China.

How glad we were when Mr. Yu (Mr. Fish) signed a contract to oversee our missionary caravan on the three-hundred mile mountainous journey north to Yaan. He had often led us on our missionary treks around the field and was a kind and reliable man. I wish I could say the same for the other men who carried the huagans and handled the horses. They were an assembly of rough men and dope addicts, all seeking the lightest load. At first they were reluctant to take the job, but the offer of generous pay won them over. They knew that people who lived along the way would taunt and ridicule them for helping the American imperialists. As we started on our journey out of Xichang they started treating us rather contemptuously, especially when crowds of people were around. This continued until we finally arrived at our destination in Yaan. Of course we couldn't blame them. They were afraid, especially when people threw stones at them.

Our route out of Xichang took us by the French Catholic Mission. What a touching scene it was as we waved goodbye to the dear old mother superior who stood at the gate of the mission smiling and waving her hand at us. She was around eighty years of age and had given the best years of her life to the work of her mission. She had left France as a young missionary nun and gone to China to serve her Lord, never to return to her homeland again. There she stood with a look of triumph on her face, expecting to die at her post in the town.

As we passed through the main gate leading north, soldiers went through the formalities of looking at our road permits, examining our baggage and being just plain obnoxious. Contempt was written all over their faces. The same thing happened at every town we passed through on our way out of the country. They kept track of us every mile of the way. In the larger towns, we were placed under an escort and told where to stay; and, after falling asleep, we were often roughly awakened during the night by soldiers insisting on seeing our road permits. They were determined to do everything they could to disturb us and make our lives miserable.

It was not enough for the soldiers along the way to bother me personally. My mule "Henry" seemed anxious to do the very same thing. I've never seen such a stubborn beast in all my life. There was no way for me to control the critter since it had no bridle. It did have a halter that could be used for leading the animal along the road but was useless when riding on its back. In the latter case, my job was to hold on to the saddle and let the horse-train handlers keep whipping Henry into line. Since my saddle was not a western saddle, I was not able to jump out of it in case of emergencies. If I leaned too much to one side, the saddle would slide right under the mule's belly. I usually mounted the animal by standing on a rock and easing myself into the saddle.

Things went along rather smoothly while we were out on the open country roads, but just as soon as we came into the towns, problems arose. The main problem was that Henry knew every horse inn and feeding place along the way and had the infernal habit of leaving the train and heading for them. Unfortunately, most of the entrances to these places had covered archways, and I was not always successful in keeping my head from being bumped as Henry surged through them. A more experienced rider could have vaulted on to the ground over Henry's hindquarters, but I was not that kind of a rider. Furthermore, after a day of riding that beast I could hardly move my legs. Most of my travel on the field was done by bicycle or foot, mostly foot. But now I was on the back of a mule that didn't like me.

On one occasion, I held on for dear life as Henry made his way through the three inner courtyards of a horse inn and entered the home of the inn keeper who had just sat down for a meal with his family. Henry walked right into the home with me crouched on his neck and stood there looking over the table, waiting for food. To say that I was embarrassed is to put it mildly. I offered a quick apology while the innkeeper welcomed me in the usual polite Chinese way, "Honorable sir, welcome to our humble home."

With a large party such as ours, we were only able to cover about fifteen miles per day. Needless to say, there were many frustrations as we tried to find accommodations in dirty little horse inns and opium dens along the way. Many of the inns couldn't handle such a large party of people. At times there was just no room in the inn for everybody.

Our first stop was in the little town of Lizhou on a rainy night, and what a stop that was. A mob of adults and children pressed in on us from every side, leaving us very little breathing space. Many of them were just plain rude. They would point their fingers at us, laugh, and shout insults. Since most Chinese do not have hair on their bodies, they delighted in pulling the hair on our arms. The children were especially curious, pawing our children and pulling their brown hair, causing them to cry in fright.

We had to push our way through this unruly crowd and stumble into our windowless room in the inn with its dirt floors and creepers and crawlers of every kind and description. Of course there were no electric lights, just crude little oil lamp holders with string wicks. Once inside, we had to lean heavily against the door in order to keep the crowd from bursting in. We remained quietly in this position until the crowd dispersed about nine o'clock at night, thinking we had fallen asleep. Then we sneaked out and bought food for our group of weary travelers. Ten children meant crumbs on the floor, but this presented no problem since we shared quarters with large hungry rats and the crumbs were all gone when we woke up the next morning.

That night the four mothers, all with babies in diapers, began what would become a daily routine on the trip. They looked for streams or begged water from innkeepers to wash out diapers and a few other necessities. The next morning they would drape them over the bamboo poles of their huagans to dry as they traveled along.

Our second stop was in our home town of Lugu, the place where we had worked so hard to win the people to Christ. Some of the people on the streets recognized us, but they were afraid to speak to us since the local officials had warned them not to do this.

After being confined to an inn for the night, we took the northern road out of town the next morning. This road led us past our cook's home. He and his family, saddened by our departure, were standing outside with tears in their eyes. Mr. Yu, the leader of our party, knew our cook well since he had often done business with us in Lugu. On several occasions he had talked to our cook after we had been escorted to Xichang and placed under house arrest. As we entered Lugu for the last time, Mr. Yu told us that our cook had really suffered under the Communists because of his relationship to us and was very poor. The bicycles and other foreign equipment that we had given him before leaving Lugu had all been confiscated and he was condemned for having accepted them. Mr. Yu asked if we could slip him some money on our way out of town. Actually, we were very low on funds; but as we passed our cook's house, Lucille quietly approached him and slipped some money into his hands. Gratitude was written all over his face as she shook his hand and then climbed back into her huagan.

Our hearts were filled with sadness as we waved goodbye to these dear friends and looked back on the town that we had loved so much. We were also saddened when we learned that Mr. Yu was forced to leave our party because of his friendliness to us. His job was turned over to a very nasty overseer who constantly showed his contempt for us as we continued our journey north.

Two days later we stopped at Mianning, the town where Ralph and I had spent nine fitful nights in the gambling den of the chief of police. How surprised we were to see our good friend, the Nosu chieftain, Lo Ziqin, sitting in the military headquarters dressed in a Communist uniform. He smiled at us, but there was no opportunity to talk to him since we were always under close surveillance. He seemed so out of place. He was the one who had told us that he would protect us from the Communists if we would move into his mountain fortress. Undoubtedly he had been pressed into wearing that uniform since he had never shown any enthusiasm for the Communist regime. We wondered what this portended for the future.

As we made our way out of Mianning the following morning and up into the high mountains, our new overseer continued to show his contempt for us. He and my mule, Henry, were one of a kind. That mule began to give me more and more trouble. I would often get off of the animal and walk along the road leading him by his halter. In fact, I was now spending more time walking than riding. Unfortunately, I was riding when we came to the lip of a waterfall. The water was about three feet deep as it poured over the cliff and straight down to the rocks about thirty or forty feet below. The stream was about thirty feet wide at this point.

Since it was too dangerous to cross the stream at this particular point, the horse train followed the stream into the mountain for about a quarter of a mile to a shallower and narrower crossing place.

But Henry had ideas of his own and, before the handlers could stop him, started out across the lip of the falls with me on his back praying for help. As I looked down at the rocks below, Henry stumbled along on the rocky stream bed and was almost across when he fell and started over the falls. I grabbed the branch of a tree that was hanging over the other side of the stream. For a moment one of my feet was caught in a stirrup and I could feel the weight of the mule pulling me over the falls when God answered my prayer. My foot slipped out of the stirrup and I made my way to shore by hanging on to the branch of that tree.

Henry was swept over the falls and kept bouncing on the rocks along the side of the cliff and on the rocks below. How he came out of that fall alive was beyond me. All I know is that when the handlers scrambled down the cliff, they found that he had made his way to shore and was lying there with cuts and bruises all over his body. They finally led him up to the road where he collapsed on the ground. The handlers beat him and forced him to get up so I could ride him. Whether I rode him or not was my problem. They certainly weren't going to cover the cost of providing another animal for me. And I certainly wasn't going to ride that suffering mule. The poor thing could only limp and was bleeding profusely, so he and I limped along the road together. I finally found myself becoming more and more attached to the poor beast. It was several days before I decided that he was sufficiently recovered for me to ride him again.

We finally made a very difficult crossing over a high mountain pass. The view of the surrounding mountains and valleys below was magnificent. Even in that time of anxiety and weariness it was a joy to see the wonders of God's handiwork. The day was rapidly coming to an end as we made our way down the other side of the mountain and found an inn in the valley below. Again the crowds gathered round and made things miserable for us as we settled down for the night. As they brushed against us, we were very conscious of the fact that the meningitis epidemic which had taken Hannah Cole was still raging in the area.

The following day we made our way through more hills and valleys and our carriers were becoming more and more belligerent and unpredictable. They would often separate themselves from the main party and take short cuts over steep terrain in order to reach the opium dens in the next town. We would often pull into a town and find our children sitting on the ground in their huagans, surrounded by crowds and crying with no one watching over them. The crowds were still giving them the same rough treatment. Where were their carriers? Smoking opium in a local den. They were altogether indifferent to our request that they travel with the main caravan and take better care of the children. They continued to act in the same foul way and their opium stops were becoming more numerous.

One day we stopped in a small town where an Army horse train had stopped. The horses were tethered to logs lying alongside the road. They were about two hundred feet up the road from us. Our carriers were smoking opium while we were buying food (usually a bowl of rice and soybean curd) at a roadside stand. We had left little Marilyn lying in her basket alongside the road. Suddenly we looked up and saw a military horse galloping down the road with its tethering log flapping at its side. Apparently someone had frightened the animal and caused it to run away. I raced to the road to move the baby out of the way, but the horse reached the basket before me. The log clipped the side of her basket and spun it around, but Marilyn was not hurt. If it had been six inches closer, she probably would have been killed.

After about ten days on the road, we came to Fulin. I wished we could have somehow bypassed the town because of the sad memories it held of Hannah Cole. All of us were filled with a sense of sadness as we settled down in a filthy rat-ridden inn and tried to find rest for our weary bodies. Of course we were under the watchful eye of the usual public security officials and they were very anxious to get rid of us.

The next morning, I decided to find Hannah's grave. We had no idea where it was located. We didn't even know if the Catholic Mission had been able to fulfill its promise to erect a memorial stone over her grave. Realizing that George and the other loved ones would like to know the same thing, I went to the city officials and asked permission to visit the grave site. At first, they said, "No," and told me to return immediately to the inn. This I refused to do. After telling them that I would report their action to the top officials when we arrived in Yaan and that I would also inform the American Embassy in Hong Kong, they granted my request. Apparently wanting to avoid an international incident, they also agreed to escort us to the grave.

I also insisted that they allow Bill Simons and me to find a local photographer to take a picture of the grave in order to prove to American officials that Hannah had been given a decent burial. Our own cameras had been confiscated long before. In that part of China, photography shops were few and far between. Even though we walked up and down the streets looking for such a shop, we had our doubts about finding one. But we felt obligated to do all that we possibly could to obtain a picture of the grave. We were just about ready to give up the search when we entered a small adobe building and found an old photographer with very little in the way of equipment. He did have, however, an old-fashioned box camera with a small supply of film.

At first, the man refused to go with us to the burial site. But the offer of a goodly amount of money for his services led to his willingness to go with us. Crowds of people jeered the photographer for being "a lowly running-dog of American imperialists" and some threw stones at him as he accompanied us along the way. Several times he was almost ready to join the crowd and curse us. But the vision of money stirred him on.

I'll never forget the walk up that hill to Hannah's grave, not because of the pebbles that children were throwing at us but because of the questions that passed through my mind. Why did Hannah have to die? Why had God allowed the Communists to take China? Why did Lee Lovegren end up in prison? Why did our son Jim have to suffer such an emotional shock? Why were we being forced to leave the field to which God had called us? Why had we seen so little in the way of a harvest?

I felt like throwing up my hands and crying out with Isaiah, "I have toiled in vain, I have spent my strength for nothing ..." (Isa. 49:4). Then we arrived at Hannah's grave. It was by the side of a lonely road next to the Catholic cemetery. A fence separated her grave from the graves of Catholics who had been buried in "holy" ground. But it certainly seemed like hallowed ground to me when I read the words carved on her tombstone: "Hannah H. Cole, 1919-1951, John 15:5." John 15:5 was Hannah's favorite verse: "I am the vine, you are the branches; he who abides in Me, and I in him, he bears much fruit; for apart from Me you can do nothing." And that was the very verse I needed at that particular time. It made all the difference in the world. It caused me to rededicate my life to Christ right there on that spot. I was in Christ; and being in Him, my labor in China had not been in vain. The seed had been sown. The harvest was in His hands. It was beneath the soil waiting to spring forth. Some of the seed had been carried by the wind to other places. Yes, I was able to say with Paul, "Now I want you to know, brethren, that my circumstances have turned out for the greater progress of the Gospel ..." (Phil. 1:12).

At first, I had dreaded the thought of stopping in Fulin. But after that visit to Hannah's grave, I was glad that I did. And I was very glad that the photographer was able to take a picture of the grave without any hindrances. We stayed in Fulin just long enough for him to develop the film and hand me the negative. He wasn't able to make a print since he had no photographic paper. With the negative safely tucked in my pack, I rushed back to the inn and joined the others who were waiting to be escorted out of town. After the routine checking of passports and baggage, we were ordered to travel north to Yaan. What a relief it was to arrive in this provincial capital about two weeks after leaving Xichang.

And what a change. From winding mountain trails to dirt roads where we saw a few old trucks and a convoy of Russian built army trucks with the conspicuous star of the Communist army on them. Here, too, we were ushered into our first decent lodging place. Instead of staying in an opium den, we were given rooms above a busy Chinese tea house where we could look out on the street below rather than trying to remain behind a closed door to keep away from the curious crowds. The guards even allowed us to cross the street to a stand where we bought some fruit that looked and tasted so good after our meager fare along those mountain trails. Of course, the toilet facilities had not changed very dramatically, but Yaan was a welcome respite. We even enjoyed the singing of a musical waiter down below who sent in his orders for tea by singing out to the cooks, "Pao cha-a-a-a-a (prepare tea)! Pao cha-a-a-a-a! Pao cha-a-a-a-a-aaaahhhhh!"

Providentially, we were able to find Ida Lovegren who was staying in a little Chinese inn in Yaan while Lee was being held in confinement. He had been sentenced to five years in prison. Ida was suffering from a bad case of malaria and looked so weary. The officials were quite angry when they learned that we had found Ida, but their anger turned to concern when we accused them of denying proper medical care to an innocent woman under their care. We insisted that she be given medical care and better food. How sad we were that the Lovegrens weren't able to join us on the road out of China. It wasn't until 1955 that Lee was released and and allowed to join Ida in Hong Kong. When Ida finally came out of China, she told us that her lot did improve soon after our departure from Yaan. They began providing medicine for her and gave her more and better food.

After a few days of rest in Yaan, we boarded a rickety bus early one morning and made a long day's journey to Chengdu where we had studied the language. After spending the night in Chengdu, we boarded another rickety bus and made the two-day journey to Chungking on the Yangtze River. By that time we were ready for the services of a chiropractor to help us unwind from the trip. But the only service available was that of an old-fashioned Chinese masseur in the rat and bedbug infested hotel to which we were assigned by the Public Security officials, and we certainly weren't anxious to have him walking all over our backs with his dirty bare feet. Added to our misery were the officials who took a great deal of delight in bothering us with their examination of our baggage and road permits.

Our three-day riverboat trip down the Yangtze River from Chungking to Hankow was very restful even though some of us had to sleep on the deck because there were not enough cabins available. Any discomforts that we might have experienced were all outweighed by the beauty of our passage through the famous Yangtze gorges.

When we arrived in Hankow, we were escorted to one of the best hotels in the city and told not to leave the hotel until we were placed on the train that would take us to Canton. This was our first nice place to stay after many days of travel. It even had modern toilet facilities. As I wandered down the main corridor, I passed a beautiful ballroom with glass chandeliers. A number of well-dressed foreign and Chinese couples were sipping cocktails and dancing to the tune of a modern band. I asked one of the bellhops to identify the people on the inside. Since he knew that I was a despised imperialist and wouldn't report him, he told me that they were members of the Russian and Chinese diplomatic corps who lived in their swank homes in a nice restricted suburb of the city.

I told him that I thought all the people in Communist China were equal. He sarcastically answered, "We, the common people, are their slaves." I'm sure this was the message that he wanted us to pass on to the people of America.

Our thirty-six-hour train ride from Hankow to Canton in southern China was without incident. Upon arrival in the city, however, the pressure was put on us again. The women were taken aside by female officials and told to lift their dresses. This was a very anxious moment for Lucille because much of this manuscript with its condemnation of the Communist regime was secretly tucked away in her underwear. The men were also made to strip. Our baggage was carefully searched. In fact, this was the most thorough search of all. Anything made in China was confiscated since it was illegal to carry such goods out of the country.

The last leg of our journey was a pleasant five-hour train ride through a beautiful rural area with its rice paddies and surrounding mountains to a small village bordering the New Territories of Greater Hong Kong. Upon arrival, we could see the British flag waving on the other side of a little bridge which separated the Territories from Communist China. Before crossing over that bridge, we had to undergo a final search and what an ordeal that was. Lucille finally sweated and prayed through it, and I was made to sweat equally as much because of what was hidden away in the bellows of my accordion. Like a fool, I had carried all of my old military papers to China with me. Numbered among them were my orders to report for duty with the Seventh Fleet in the Pacific. And this was the fleet keeping the Chinese Communists out of Formosa (Taiwan). I dreaded the thought of what might happen to my family and the other families if they found those orders inside the bellows of my accordion. After thirty one days on the road, were we going to end up in a Communist prison?

"HE THEN BROUGHT ME OUT ..." 231

The only piece of equipment I tried to carry out of China was my accordion. All of our other possessions had been left behind or confiscated. I trembled when an inspector came up to me and told me to open up the bellows of the instrument. I was in the process of removing the screws from the bellows when my inspector was called away by another inspector who wanted his help. When he returned about a half hour later, he had forgotten all about opening the accordion and approved our crossing over that little bridge to freedom.

Only those who have gone through similar experiences can appreciate the depth of emotion that surged through us as we crossed that bridge. We laughed and cried and shouted with joy. We breathed deeply. The straitjacket was gone. We could open our mouths and say what we wanted to say. No one was listening. The Union Jack waived in the breeze proclaiming freedom! We were quickly transported to the very modern Four Seas Hotel. We all acted like little children when we entered our spotless and spacious accomodations with comfortable beds, lovely bed spreads, private bath rooms, telephones and laundry service. It seemed just like Heaven! But after looking at our road-worn and tramp-like appearance in the mirror, we felt as though we didn't belong there. That feeling soon disappeared as we jumped into bathtubs, scrubbed ourselves, and then donned new clothing purchased on the streets of Hong Kong. How we thanked the Lord for answering our prayers. He safely brought us out through "THE GATE FACING EAST" and than led us to Taiwan where we served Him for many more years.

After twenty-five years of service with the Conservative Baptist Foreign Mission Society, I who had questioned my calling found it necessary to resign from the mission because of my physical condition. The same situation had faced me twenty-five years before when I was hospitalized back to the States after serving as a chaplain in the Philippines.

A number of years later Janet, my youngest daughter who was born in Taiwan, asked me a question. At that time, she and her husband, Roger Twining, were teaching at a local school. This was her question, "Dad, do you believe a call to be a missionary is more important than a call to be a teacher?" This was my reply, "It's not a question of which calling is more important. In God's sight, both calls are important. It's a question of, HOW FAITHFUL ARE WE IN FULFILLING OUR CALLING?"

Pinyin Alphabet Pronunciation Guide

a Vowel as in *far*
b Consonant as in *be*
c Consonant as in *its*
ch Consonant as in *chip*; strongly aspirated
d Consonant as in *do*
e Vowel as in *her*
f Consonant as in *foot*
g Consonant as in *go*
h Consonant as in *her*; strongly aspirated
i Vowel as in *eat* or as in *sir* (when in syllables beginning with c, ch, r, s, sh, z, and zh)
j Consonant as in *jeep*
k Consonant as in *kind*; strongly aspirated
l Consonant as in *lard*
m Consonant as in *me*
o Vowel as in *law*
p Consonant as in *par*; strongly aspirated
q Consonant as in *cheek*
r Consonant as in *right* (not rolled) or pronounced z as in *azure*
s Consonant as in *sister*
sh Consonant as in *shore*
t Consonant as in *top*; strongly aspirated
u Vowel as in *too*; also as in French *tu* or the German *Munchen*
v Consonant used only to produce foreign words, national minority words, and local dialects
w Semi-vowel in syllables beginning with u when not preceded by consonants, as in *want*
x Consonant as in *she*
y Semi-vowel in syllables beginning with i or u when not preceded by consonants, as in *yet*
z Consonant as in *zero*
zh Consonant as in *jump*

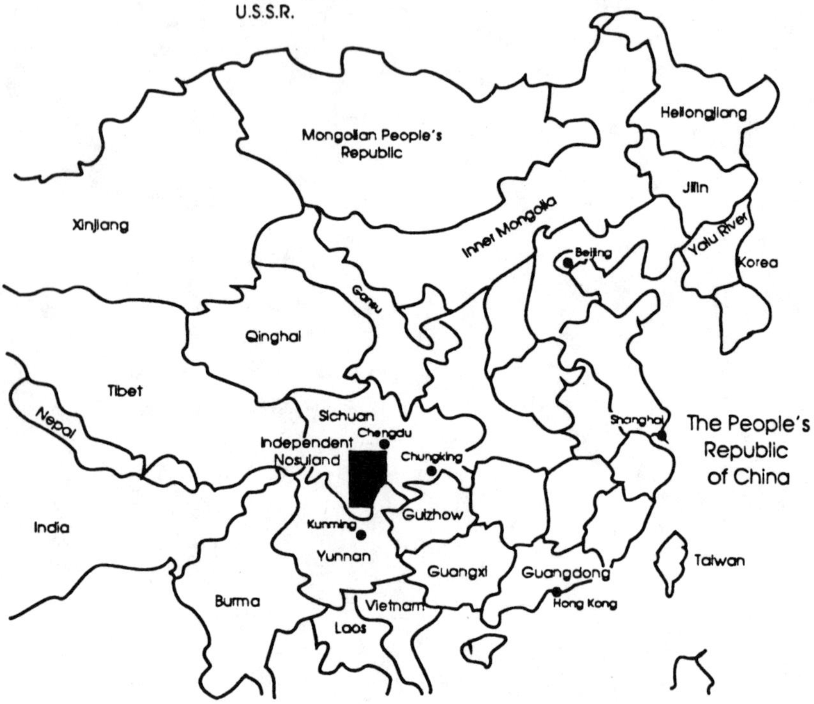
U.S.S.R.
Mongolian People's Republic
Heilongjiang
Jilin
Inner Mongolia
Xinjiang
Beijing
Yalu River
Korea
Gansu
Qinghai
Tibet
Nepal
Sichuan
Chengdu
Independent Nosuland
Chungking
Shanghai
The People's Republic of China
Guizhow
Kunming
India
Yunnan
Guangxi
Guangdong
Taiwan
Hong Kong
Burma
Vietnam
Laos